SUBLIMATION

SUBLIMATION

Inquiries into Theoretical Psychoanalysis

HANS W. LOEWALD, M.D.

YALE UNIVERSITY PRESS

NEW HAVEN AND LONDON

Designed by Jo Aerne and set in Electra type with
Futura for display by Huron Valley Graphics.
Printed in the United States of America by Halliday
Lithograph, West Hanover, Massachusetts.

Library of Congress Cataloging-in-Publication Data
Loewald, Hans, W., 1906–
Sublimation : inquiries into theoretical
psychoanalysis.
Bibliography: p.   Includes index.
1. Sublimation. 2. Psychoanalysis. I. Title.
BF175.5.S92L64 1988   150.19′5   88–14271
ISBN 0–300–04234–5 (alk. paper)

10 9 8 7 6 5 4 3 2 1

A second outcome of the work of psycho-analysis is that it then becomes possible for the unconscious instincts revealed by it to be employed for the useful purposes which they would have found earlier if development had not been interrupted. For the extirpation of the infantile wishful impulses is by no means the ideal aim of development. Owing to their repressions, neurotics have sacrificed many sources of mental energy whose contributions would have been of great value in the formation of their character and in their activity in life. We know of a far more expedient process of development, called *'sublimation'*, in which the energy of the infantile wishful impulses is not cut off but remains ready for use—the unserviceable aim of the various impulses being replaced by one that is higher, and perhaps no longer sexual. It happens to be precisely the components of the *sexual* instinct that are specially marked by a capacity of this kind for sublimation, for exchanging their sexual aim for another one which is comparatively remote and socially valuable. It is probable that we owe our highest cultural successes to the contributions of energy made in this way to our mental functions. Premature repression makes the sublimation of the repressed impulse impossible; when the repression is lifted, the path to sublimation becomes free once more.

Sigmund Freud, "Five Lectures on Psycho-Analysis"

C O N T E N T S

PREFACE

It is a sobering and strangely comforting thought that writing these investigations has been a sublimated way of cleaning and preening myself, like a cat after a meal, or after a frustrating hunt. Perhaps this thought counterbalances a certain one-sidedness in my presentation: it may be that there is more embellishment and self-exoneration—which Freud saw as an important part of sublimation—in my account than I had been aware of.

The book, short as it is, was written over a period of several years, with many long interruptions due to other work and to life circumstances beyond my control.

In 1981, under the auspices of the Western New England Institute for Psychoanalysis, I conducted a series of seminars on sublimation with a small group of candidates and graduates of the institute. The literature reports they contributed and their active and stimulating participation in the seminar discussions were of great help to me. So were discussions at several professional meetings where I presented some of the material contained in the following pages. To my regret, I have been able to deal here with only a few psychoanalytic writings on the topic. But I wish to record my special indebtedness to the work of Ernst Kris—not only on sublimation but also on many related subjects.

A word on the subtitle is in order. I use so-called metapsychological concepts and terms in the following investigations. But I believe that the term *metapsychology*, except in historical context, has outlived its usefulness. It is redundant in this day and age, if one holds to Freud's original meaning—that is, psychology that goes beyond the psychology of consciousness—because psychology as including the unconscious is now by and large taken for granted, in contrast to the time when Freud first coined the term. Later on, especially in Freud's "metapsychological" papers, the term referred to the general theory of psychoanalysis as a scientific discipline. Metapsychology, in this sense of the word, does not go beyond psychology as empirical science any more than theoretical physics and theoretical biology go beyond physics and biology qua observational and experimental sciences. The specifically theoretical branches of a science search for the fundamental conceptual premises embedded in empirical knowledge and for conceptual innovations that may influence or change that knowledge. Thus, I use the term *theoretical psychoanalysis*, in analogy to the terms *theoretical physics* and *theoretical biology*, in order to indicate the scope of my inquiries. I introduce this new name without any implication that what has gone under the title *metapsychology* is inimical to, or is not, psychoanalytic psychology.

New Haven, Connecticut
October 1987

SUBLIMATION

INTRODUCTION

Sublimation, to the psychoanalyst, is at once privileged and suspect. Its privileged status is due to human self-valuation: we take for granted the uniqueness of our psychic life and development; the value of man's imagination and thought, creativity and civilization; the worth of cultural pursuits—of morality, religion, the arts and sciences, and philosophy—and of an organized, self-reflective conduct of personal life and life in society. Sublimation appears to be operative in all these developments and pursuits.

Sublimation is suspect insofar as psychoanalysis, from the vantage point of instinctual-unconscious mentation, tends to regard more differentiated or "further advanced" modes of psychic life as defensive, even illusory in nature, as concealments or more or less intriguing, fanciful embellishments of the elementary, true psychic reality of instinctual-unconscious life. These elaborations and advances themselves are thus ultimately to be understood as motivated by unconscious wishes whose aims are quite different from those higher aims—so dear to us—that human consciousness perceives in them.

As early as the 1890s, in the Fliess papers, where sublimation makes its first appearance on the psychoanalytic scene, Freud clearly foreshadowed its ambiguous character. He speaks there of *phantasies* as "psychical façades constructed in order to bar the way to these memories"—memories, that is, of what he calls "primal scenes." He argues that "phantasies at the same time serve the trend towards refining the memories, towards sublimating them" (Freud 1892–99, Draft L [1897], p. 248). In a letter to Fliess of the same date he describes phantasies as "protective structures [*Schutzbauten*], sublimations of the facts, embellishments of them, and at the same time [they] serve for self-exoneration" (ibid., Letter 61 [1897], p. 247). At another point in the same letter he speaks of phantasies as *Schutzdich-tungen*, protective fictions (p. 248). Memories here are veridical records of facts (specifically of primal scenes), and phantasies arise to protect against them as well as to refine, to sublimate them.

When it comes to the nature of "facts," of reality, that too is ambiguous in psychoanalysis. In *The Interpretation of Dreams* Freud distinguished between psychical reality and material or factual reality. But he did not commit himself unequivocally to attributing reality even to unconscious wishes, despite their closeness to material (in the sense of neurobiological) reality. "Whether we are to attribute *reality* to unconscious wishes, I cannot say. It must be denied, of course, to any transitional or intermediate thoughts. If we look at unconscious wishes reduced to their most fundamental and truest shape, we shall have to conclude, no doubt, that *psychical* reality is a particular form of existence not to be confused with *material* reality" (1900, p. 620; Freud's italics). The "reality" of the unconscious, as a "particular form of existence," is affirmed and in doubt at the same time. Given Freud's commitment to scientific materialism as well as to the scientific investigation of that "particular form of existence" which is "immaterial," he was forced to straddle the issue. Psychoanalysis has remained on the fence, but it can no longer in good conscience stay wedded to scientific materialism, in view of the developments of scientific and philosophical investigations and thought in the twentieth century.[1]

It is also significant that for Freud, from a Kantian perspective, "reality will always remain 'unknowable' " (1940[1938], p. 196). And this goes for material as well as for psychic reality. Toward the end of his life, in "An Outline of Psychoanalysis," he writes: "In our science as in the others [like physics] the problem is the same: behind the attributes (qualities) of the object under examination which are presented directly to our perception, we have to discover something else

1. By *scientific materialism* I understand here "a widely held system of thought that explains the nature of the world as entirely dependent on matter, the fundamental and final reality beyond which nothing need be sought" (*The New Columbia Encyclopedia*, 4th ed., s. v. "materialism").

2

which is more independent of the particular receptive capacity of our sense organs and which approximates more closely to what may be supposed to be the real state of affairs. We have no hope of being able to reach the latter itself." (1940 [1938], p. 196). The true psychic reality of unconscious-instinctual life is the subjective counterpart to the true objective external reality, both unknowable in themselves. The id is the ego's "second external world" (see Freud 1923b, p. 55). Here reality, whether "physical" or "psychical," is defined as external to the ego and having to submit to the ego, to be modified by it, or both. There are a number of indications in Freud's writings, from early to late ones, that the difference between psychic reality (instinct-unconscious) and material reality tends to collapse as one gets closer "to what may be supposed to be the real state of affairs." The status of the ego, and with it the status of sublimation, remains even more enigmatic than that.

The idea of reality, in the sense of some underlying, absolute, "objective" truth, has itself become problematic since Freud. Nevertheless, the scientific discipline of psychoanalysis implicitly posits the totality of the individual's psychic life—unconscious and conscious—as real, in the sense that it is assumed to be a legitimate subject for unprejudiced, systematic "analytic" investigation and to be sufficiently distinct in our apprehension from other forms of existence to make such investigation possible. Ultimately, psychic life is real for psychoanalysis insofar as this form of existence constitutes the power and validity of man as human.

Traditionally, sublimation is classified in psychoanalysis as *defense*. Freud did not see it as pathogenic or pathological—quite the contrary. Otto Fenichel distinguished between successful and unsuccessful defenses and assigned pathogenic defenses to the second category. He wrote: "The successful defenses may be placed under the heading sublimation [which term] does not designate a specific [defense] mechanism. . . . The common factor is that under the influence of the ego, aim or object (or both) is changed without blocking an adequate discharge" (Fenichel 1945, p. 141). In subsequent references to sublimation, Fenichel speaks of channelizing impulses (p. 153) and of the ego forming "a channel and not a dam for the instinctual stream" (pp. 470–71). A careful reading of Fenichel's discussions—especially on the relations between ego formation, character formation, and sublimation—shows that a distinction between ego formation and sublimation is not easily made and that the psychoanalytic concept of defense is ambiguous (on both these issues see also Hartmann 1955, pp. 16–17).

The concept of defense, on the one hand, comprises everything that in some way does not conform to what is postulated as the inherent pressure for discharge of an instinctual current, regardless of the specific nature of such a deviation from the assumed natural course of events. On the other hand, the more narrow reference of the term *defense* is to only those processes, or "mechanisms," that dam up, block, or run against the instinctual stream and that take the form of "countercathexes" erected or maintained by the ego. One may formulate the difference in the following simplified way: In the latter case the ego *uses* defensive functions—which, among other functions, it has available—against the id; this may or may not lead to pathology, depending on a variety of factors. In the former, far more comprehensive meaning of defense, the ego as an organization—although not per se pathological or pathogenic in a clinical sense—is in its very nature and purpose a defense structure posed against the id. Defense against the id is not understood here as one of the ego's functions that it may call into play; rather, ego is defined as defense structure, a structure designed, as it were, to disguise or impede the true psychic reality represented by the id. The limited concept of defense is relevant for the understanding of repression and similar mechanisms operating in normal life and neurosis.[2] The comprehensive defense concept does not

2. It must be realized, however, that frequently in the psychoanalytic literature, including works by Freud himself, the very distinction between the terms *repression* and *defense* has been blurred, inasmuch as *repression* often is used interchangeably

discriminate between higher psychic organization and defense but explains higher organization as a defense. It is based ultimately on a priori assumptions regarding the "aim" of instinctual impulses and the rule of the inertia or constancy principle (the "unpleasure principle"), assumptions that are highly questionable. Freud himself eventually became doubtful about them: he began to change his views on the nature of pleasure and introduced the life-instinct concept. Without going further into these fundamental matters at this point, it will be useful to keep in mind that a distinction may be made between processes that dam up, countercathect instinctual life and processes that channel and organize it.

What is it that is being changed in the process called sublimation? The answer, according to original psychoanalytic theory, is the sexual instincts (drives) or libidinal impulses. (The introduction of aggression as a basic instinct different from sexuality—bringing with it the problem of sublimation of aggressive impulses—occurs only in later versions of psychoanalytic theory). How sublimatory transformations of instincts come about, what they consist of, what "agency" (or agencies) put them into effect—these are central questions we will pursue. But it is important to realize from the beginning that in psychoanalysis qua developmental theory, the term *sublimation* implies transformation of instincts. In his encyclopedia article "The Libido Theory" (1923a), Freud states: "Psychoanalysis early became aware that all mental occurrences must be regarded as built on the basis of an interplay of the forces of the elementary instincts" (p. 255). If the libido theory taken in this general sense is abandoned— if, let us say, primacy of self, in contrast to primacy of libido, is stipulated—then the meaning of the concept sublimation vanishes, to give way, perhaps, to a creationist view of the world.

Freud and later theoreticians have debated whether the term

---

with *defense*, or even is substituted for the latter term, and thus tends to gain the status of the comprehensive defense concept.

should be reserved for those phenomena implicated in the higher, or more highly valued, human functions and creations—with cultural, religious, moral, and artistic attainments and purposes—or whether it should refer to all psychic functioning that goes beyond the unmediated pursuit of direct instinct discharge without being affected, as in the case of the "unsuccessful defenses" of Fenichel, by unresolved conflict and defenses against that discharge. In practice we often speak of sublimation in the first sense. But as soon as one tries to clarify theoretically what is involved in sublimation, it seems likely that the psychic processes we deal with in those "higher" pursuits are not essentially different from those we encounter in the formation of ego and superego and in character formation in general, as contrasted with what we regard as primitive instinctual life.

The relationship between sublimation and culture, or civilization,[3] is complex. Freud sometimes spoke of civilization as "a peculiar process which mankind undergoes" (1930, p. 96), "comparable to the normal maturation of the individual" (p. 98)—in other words, as a quasi-biological process undergone by the human race in the course of evolution. He also wrote, in the same context.

> Sublimation of instinct is an especially conspicuous feature of cultural development; it is what makes it possible for higher psychical activities, scientific, artistic or ideological, to play such an important part in civilized life. If one were to yield to a first impression, one would say that sublimation is a vicissitude which has been forced upon the

3. Freud resisted the distinction frequently made in German between *Kultur* and *Zivilisation*. The main reason was, I believe, that he opposed the value judgment implied for many Germans, at least of his era, in that distinction: *Kultur* was something exalted that had to do with high moral standards, higher education, the arts and the humanities, and refined tastes and sensibilities; and it had elitist overtones. *Zivilisation* tended to be used in referring to the more earthbound, practical accomplishments of mankind, such as the development of tools, agriculture, technologies, and so forth—achievements related to practical necessity and utility which had pragmatic worth but not the spiritual value and appeal of *Kultur*. Thus, for Freud the German distinction was tainted by just those pretensions that made sublimation suspect.

instincts entirely by civilization. But it would be wiser to reflect upon this a little longer. (Ibid., p. 97)

Further reflection suggests, for one thing, that civilization itself does not emerge without the contributions of sublimatory "aim inhibition" and "object displacement." Once the results of such processes have come about, in the form of more civilized life, they gain a momentum of their own and influence further individual development. Nevertheless, in itself, sublimatory transformation of instinct seems indebted to "civilizing" constraints coming from parents, models, teachers—in short, to educational experiences in the broad sense. This circularity points to the familiar problem of mutually facilitating—or interfering—reciprocal interactions between individual and environment, and their internalization by the individual, which then helps to shape or reshape the civilizing environment.

The consideration of civilization as a kind of organic process undergone by mankind is related to Freud's speculations about "organic repression" (1930, pp. 99–100, n. 1) brought about by our ancestors' change to the upright posture, as well as to his argument that the repression and destruction present in the Oedipus complex is determined by heredity and the biphasic development of sexuality in humans (1924b, pp. 173–74). One might then speculate about a parallel to organic repression: "organic sublimation." Such speculations are not so far-fetched if we consider that latency and adolescence are stages in psychosexual development that follow biological upsurges of sexuality and are distinguished, it seems, by heightened sublimatory, not merely repressive, activity. It is often thought that sublimation and its effects are first clearly observable during latency and again prominently in adolescence.

In sum, the notion of sublimation comes readily to mind in psychoanalytic theory whenever it tries to explicate the emergence and presence of specifically human functions and productions and the psychic structures related to them, those which bespeak a complex level of mental functioning, which have a positive significance for us, and which are considered nonpathological. Freud often thought of sublimation as a capacity—not greatly developed in the majority of people—that is conducive to mental health, if not indispensable for it. The term, no matter how poorly understood and elaborated, points to something exceedingly important to mankind. Without this something—tentatively conceived as a form of transformation from primitive to more advanced levels of mentation—without these transmuting processes and capacities, man would not be man. When psychoanalysts consider human creativity, whether on the plane of daily living and ordinary work or on the plane of higher cultural pursuits and original thought and imagination, they have recourse to the idea of sublimation. The psychoanalyst's work itself and that of his patients in the therapeutic process involve and require sublimatory activity, the capacity for and activation of these contained and containing, yet releasing, transformations we wish to understand better.

I have sketched only some of the problems of sublimation that will be discussed in the following pages. The exploration will proceed along often diverging and sometimes conflicting paths and will involve reformulations and revisions of some fundamental theoretical concepts. Consequently some clinical phenomena and observations will be seen in a different light. My method of approach will be unsystematic; I shall not develop a straight and continuous line of argument. Instead, I shall try to elucidate the subject matter by describing it from various angles and perspectives and by adopting diverse modes and moods of discourse. If this leads the reader to conclude that I contradict myself at some crucial points, so be it. Truth is not absolute or one-directional. Contradiction, conflict, spiraling, reconciliation, a dissolving of achieved reconciliations, new resolutions of dissonances—these are at the center of life and the mind's life, and of the topic of this inquiry.

CHAPTER ONE

Transformations of Passion

and Their Vicissitudes

Sublimation is passion transformed. Freud described Leonardo da Vinci's mental activity in these terms:

> His affects were controlled and subjected to the instinct for research; he did not love and hate, but asked himself about the origin and significance of what he was to love or hate. Thus he was bound at first to appear indifferent to good and evil, beauty and ugliness. During his work of investigation love and hate threw off their positive or negative signs and were both alike transformed into intellectual interest. In reality Leonardo was not devoid of passion; he did not lack the divine spark which is directly or indirectly the driving force—*il primo motore*—behind all human activity. He had merely converted his passion into a thirst for knowledge; he then applied himself to investigation with the persistence, constancy and penetration which is derived from passion, and at the climax of intellectual labour, when knowledge had been won, he allowed the long restrained affect to break loose and to flow away freely, as a stream of water drawn from a river is allowed to flow away when its work is done. When, at the climax of a discovery, he could survey a large portion of the whole nexus, he was overcome by emotion, and in ecstatic language praised the splendour of the part of creation that he had studied, or—in

religious phraseology—the greatness of his Creator. (1910b, p. 74–75)[1]

Here is another passage from Freud's essay on Leonardo:

> Originally the genitals were the pride and hope of living beings; they were worshipped as gods and transmitted the divine nature of their functions to all newly learned human activities. As a result of the sublimation of their basic nature there arose innumerable divinities; and at the time when the connection between official religions and sexual activity was already hidden from the general consciousness, secret cults devoted themselves to keeping it alive among a number of initiates. In the course of cultural development so much of the divine and sacred was ultimately extracted from sexuality that the exhausted remnant fell into contempt. (1910b, p. 97)[2]

1. Since the *Standard Edition* translation of this passage (as of the one that follows) is unsatisfactory in some respects, quotation of the German text is indicated: "Seine Affekte waren gebaendigt, dem Forschertrieb unterworfen; er liebte und hasste nicht, sondern fragte sich, woher das komme, was er lieben oder hassen solle, und was es bedeute, und so musste er zunaechst indifferent erscheinen gegen Gut und Boese, gegen Schoenes und Haessliches. Waehrend dieser Forscherarbeit warfen Liebe und Hass ihre Vorzeichen ab und wandelten sich gleichmaessig in Denkinteresse um. In Wirklichkeit war Leonardo nicht leidenschaftslos, er enbehrte nicht des goettlichen Funkens, der mittelbar oder unmittelbar die Triebkraft—*il primo motore*—alles menschlichen Tuns ist. Er hatte die Leidenschaft nur in Wissensdrang verwandelt; er ergab sich nun der Forschung mit jener Ausdauer, Stetigkeit, Vertiefung, die sich aus der Leidenschaft ableiten, und auf der Hoehe der geistigen Arbeit, nach gewonnener Erkenntnis, laesst er den lange zuruekgehaltenen Affekt losbrechen, frei abstroemen wie einen vom Strome abgeleiteten Wasserarm, nachdem er das Werk getrieben hat. Auf der Hoehe einer Erkenntnis, wenn er ein grosses Stueck des Zusammenhanges ueberschauen kann, dann erfasst ihn das Pathos und er preist in schwaermerischen Worten die Grossartigkeit jenes Stueckes der Schoepfung, das er studiert hat, oder—in religioeser Einkleidung—die Groesse seines Schoepfers" (*Gesammelte Werke* 8:141). The German text is more vivid and poignant and more precise. This is especially noticeable in a study which is written in a rather free-flowing style and in which Freud's personal engagement shines through so clearly.

2. Short of giving the whole passage in German, I can point out only that the word *transmitted* in the second part of the first sentence is better translated as *transferred*. *Uebertrugen* is the perfect tense of *uebertragen* (as in *Uebertragung*, "transference"). G. W., 8: 166–67.

This passage alludes to a side of Freud's conception of sexuality that he generally kept under wraps and that he did not include in his theoretical thought until he formulated his last instinct theory.[3]

Eros, the life or love instinct, is clearly invoked in both passages. In the first, it is called the divine spark, *il primo motore* of all human activity. In the second passage Freud speaks of the divine and sacred nature of sexual functions and its transference to all newly learned human activities, and of the genitals as "the pride and hope" of the living. Divinities rose out of their basic nature by sublimation, separated-out and exalted elements of sexuality which still remain within its sweep. Then follows the sentence on the course of cultural development: So much of the divine and sacred was extracted from sexuality that it fell into disrepute, an "exhausted remnant" no longer containing and evoking the divine. Freud is suggesting that it is a disruption within the full nature or scope of sexuality that leads to increasing disconnection between sexuality and the divine. To the extent that the course of cultural development (of both the race and the individual) leads to sexuality's being emptied of the divine— which thus becomes more and more disembodied—both sexuality and the divine are impoverished. The discontents of civilization include not only the starvation and denigration of instinctual life but, one must conclude, the impoverishment of the divine, of spirituality, as well; as it progresses, the disruption of the original oneness of sexuality and the divine deprives both of meaning. It is here that the

3. Jung was well aware of, and even in awe of, that side. In *Memories, Dreams, Reflections* (1963) he wrote: "There was no mistaking the fact that Freud was emotionally involved in his sexual theory to an extraordinary degree. When he spoke of it, his tone became urgent, almost anxious, and all signs of his normally critical and skeptical manner vanished. A strange, deeply moved expression came over his face, the cause of which I was at a loss to understand" (p. 150). And later: "Just as the psychically stronger agency [the Unconscious] is given 'divine' or 'daemonic' attributes, so the 'sexual libido' took over the role of a *deus absconditus*, a hidden or concealed god" (p. 151). Here Jung reflected on conversations he had with Freud in 1907 and in 1910 (the year when the essay on Leonardo was published).

death instinct shows its silent power. In genuine sublimation, I suggest, that disruption is not dominant, or is overcome.

Freud spoke of the divine nature of sexual functions as being *transferred* to all newly learned human activities (Strachey's version is "transmitted"; see note 2, above). I doubt that he used the word casually. The connection of sublimation and transference was already made in the postscript to the Dora case. There, likening some transferences to facsimiles and others to new editions of earlier impulses or phantasies, he explained that the content of new editions "has been subjected to a moderating influence—to *'sublimation'* as I call it" (1905, p. 116; Freud's emphasis). He explains that these transferences are revisions (*Neubearbeitungen*), not mere reprints (*Neudrucke*).

According to the *Oxford English Dictionary* (O.E.D.), the primary sense of the word *sublimation* is as follows: "The chemical action or process of subliming or converting a solid substance by means of heat into vapour, which resolidifies on cooling." This usage was first recorded in the fourteenth century. In a figurative (should one say, "sublimated"?) sense it began to be used in the seventeenth century and is defined by the O.E.D. as "elevation to a higher state or plane of existence; transmutation into something higher, purer, or more sublime." The etymology of the word *sublime* suggests rising to a limit or upper threshold and proceeding on a slope. Its familiar use as an adjective or noun (*the sublime*) is preceded by its use as a verb: to sublime means to sublimate in the chemical sense. In "The Canon's Yeoman's Tale," Chaucer decries the attempts of medieval alchemists to sublime, or transmute base metals into gold (*The Canterbury Tales* [ca. 1387–1400]). The canon's engagement in these activities is described as ridiculous and corrupt—stigmas that the sublime and sublimation somehow cannot quite shake off: there always lurks the possibility or suspicion that there is something laughable, effete, or not genuine about them. *Sublimation*, in both the chemical and the psychoanalytic senses, denotes some sort of conversion or transmutation from a lower to a higher, and presumably purer, state or plane of existence—be it the transmutation of a material substance or of an instinct and its objects and aims. The psychoanalytic term *conversion* designates transformation in the opposite direction, that is, from higher levels of psychic functioning to a lower level manifested only in somatic form. This process ordinarily is attributed to repression. Conversion and other forms of somatization, for example, psychosomatic disorder, appear to be opposites of sublimation.

We tend to think automatically of transmutation from lower to higher levels as a form of progression from coarse, crude states or processes to more refined, advanced ones that have given up, and left behind, their primitive, crude origins. In the second quotation from the Leonardo study Freud suggests a different vista: The "lowest" and "highest" are enveloped as one within an original unitary experience; one *is* the other, and later they can stand for one another, the body and its powers a symbol of the godhead, the deity a symbol of the living sexual body. It is the original unity that is in the process of being restored, or something of it is saved, in sublimation; there is a symbolic *linkage* which constitutes what we call meaning (later on I shall discuss symbolism more extensively). In such a view, the transmutations of sublimation reveal an unfolding into differentiated elements of a oneness of instinctual-spiritual experience: oneness stays alive as connection. Sublimations are progressing differentiations that culminate in new synthetic organizations of such unitary experiences. The elements we call *instinctual* and *deinstinctualized* each acquire a measure of autonomy without losing the other. Psychoanalysis, in this view, does not uncover the truth of objective reality behind illusive higher levels of experience (so that the genitals and their power would constitute the true unadorned reality hidden beneath the disguising symbol of a god). Instead, by juxtaposing the two elements of an original unity and emphasizing the one hidden and defended against, psychoanalysis aims at showing their hidden linkage. The "secondary process" has differentiated the elements in the first place; psychoanalysis reveals the inextricable bond of primary and secondary process. It was a main thrust of Freud's work to rescue sexuality, that "exhausted remnant" of cultural development, from intellectual and moral oblivion and contempt. He recognized that sublimation becomes a sham when the vital links, evoking an ancient identity, of the "highest" and "lowest" in human nature are repressed.

The unitary experience of which I spoke has been described—speaking in terms of individual development—as the undifferentiated phase of psychic development, as contrasted with the notion that the primary given is the id, out of which the ego develops. For a fuller understanding of sublimation, I emphasize that in this first phase there is likewise no differentiation of subject and object, of a self and an object world. The essential part this emerging differentiation plays in sublimation is the topic to which I now turn.

CHAPTER TWO

Theoretical Advances

This chapter will be concerned with psychoanalytic theory and metapsychology relevant to sublimation.[1] I hope this will serve—in addition to the immediate purpose—the aim of preserving and strengthening the symbolic links between the concrete and the abstract, of staving off the impoverishment of abstract theory, which leads to its falling into contempt and being discarded easily. Theory, too, is a work and product of sublimation. If it loses vitality because it has become too remote from concrete experience, or because we no longer make the effort required to understand the presence of abstraction and theory in the life of our science (as of any science) and in our clinical work, we are in danger of losing the subject matter along with the theory.

A crucial landmark in the development of the concept of

1. I use the term *metapsychology* here in the fairly broad sense Freud adopts in a footnote to the title of his paper "A Metapsychological Supplement to the Theory of Dreams" (1917a). He writes: "The two following papers [this one and "Mourning and Melancholia"] are connected with the preceding ones ["Instincts and Their Vicissitudes," "Repression," and "The Unconscious"] and derive from a collection which I originally wanted to publish under the title 'Preliminaries to a Metapsychology.' The intention of this series is to clarify and carry deeper the theoretical assumptions on which one could found a psychoanalytic system." (I have modified Strachey's translation; compare *S.E.* 14:222 and *G.W.* 10:412.)

There are, of course, other aspects to *metapsychology* as Freud and later authors used the term. A discussion of these various meanings, not attempted here, would show the complexity of, as well as a degree of confusion in, psychoanalytic thought beginning with Freud in regard to fundamental matters of theory formation. (See the article on metapsychology in Laplanche and Pontalis 1967 for a survey.)

sublimation—as of a number of other metapsychological concepts—was the introduction of the concept of *narcissism* into libido and instinct theory. Therefore I shall discuss sublimation first from that vantage point, turning later to other perspectives from which sublimation can be and has been viewed. With the formulation and elaboration of the narcissism concept, ego psychology began to come into its own. I am not thinking here of the shift of emphasis from id psychology to ego functions, defenses, and adaptation but of the more essential shift to an analysis of the ego in terms of the genetic-dynamic construction of psychic organization or structure. Freud addresses this aspect of ego psychology—the *depth psychology of the ego*—mainly in "Mourning and Melancholia" (1917b) and in parts of *Beyond the Pleasure Principle* (1920), *Group Psychology and the Analysis of the Ego* (1921), and *The Ego and the Id* (1923b). The groundwork had been laid previously in *Totem and Taboo* (1913b) and "On Narcissism" (1914). In the first chapter of *Civilization and Its Discontents* (1930) Freud further develops the concept of primary narcissism. Libido theory and ego theory become inseparable: a depth psychology of the ego comes into being with the new distinctions between narcissistic libido and object libido and, correspondingly, between identification and object cathexis. Once narcissistic libido and object libido had been distinguished and the concept of primary narcissism revised, other theoretical changes followed:

    1. Libido and sexuality were conceived as encompassing not only object relations but also the cohesive fabric of intrapsychic structure (the internal binding and uniting of eros). The term *libido* previously had a narrow denotation, that is, simply object libido (even if "autoerotic"). In other words, now it was not only the relations and interactions of subject and object that were seen as based on instinctual, sexual-aggressive impulses; so too were the internal relations and interactions constituting the organization of the subject as a psychic entity or structured unit. This widening of the definition of sexuality culminated in Freud's concept of eros, the life or love instinct.

2. Primary narcissism was first identified as "the great reservoir of libido" (Freud 1923, pp. 46, 63 ff.), from which a part flows out to objects and can secondarily return to the reservoir (secondary narcissism); another part always stays in the reservoir. Freud vacillated between assigning this reservoir to the ego (as a substructure of the *Gesamt-Ich*, or "total subject," or self) versus assigning it to the id; an indecision that reflects the large role he believed narcissism played in providing the instinctual basis for ego. The idea of object libido returning to the reservoir, of the setting- up of the object in the ego (that is, narcissistic identification) led to the specification of *internalization* as the path for ego development.

In *Civilization and Its Discontents* Freud tries out a further step, namely, to understand primary narcissism as that primal state where id-ego and external world are not differentiated: narcissistic and object libido differentiate out of a stage where ego and object and their cathexes are as yet not distinguished or distinguishable (see Freud 1930, pp. 64–73, especially, p. 68 and pp. 72–73). Such a view, entertained by Freud only reluctantly, differs from the explanation of primary narcissism given in *The Ego and the Id*, where the concept means that all libido is originally contained in the ego and then emanates "to objects." Differentiating processes, which I have conceptualized as primary internalizations and externalizations (Loewald [1962] 1980, pp. 265–66), lead to the formation both of id-ego and of objects, the two more or less distinct from each other, and to the differentiation of narcissistic and object libido.[2]

2. It must be acknowledged that the term *primary narcissism* is imprecise and confusing when used to designate the absence of subject-object differentiation. *Narcissistic* usually refers to that portion of libido which displays itself within the subject. Cathexis could be neither narcissistic nor object-directed without subject-object differentiation. The word *narcissism* is used to designate that primal stage of nondifferentiation insofar as we prospectively focus on the emergence out of that stage of ego, or self, rather than of the object world. Similarly, psychoanalysis often speaks of *object relations* in a sense that includes identifications, although at early stages object cathexis and identification are not yet differentiated from one another. These are confusing

These primary internalizations and externalizations are followed by those with which we are more familiar from our understanding of superego development. Internalization on that level was described—although not so named—by Freud when he discussed ego-ideal formation in *Group Psychology and the Analysis of the Ego* (1921): "The ego now enters into the relation of an object to the ego ideal which has been developed out of it, and . . . all the interplay between an external object and the ego as a whole, with which our study of the neuroses has made us acquainted, may possibly be repeated upon this new scene of action within the ego" (p. 130).

In the course of discussing superego formation in *The Ego and the Id*, he speaks of this transposition onto a new, internal scene of action as "transformation of an erotic object-choice into an alteration of the ego" (1923b, p. 30). He continues a few sentences further as follows:

> The transformation of object-libido into narcissistic libido which thus takes place obviously implies an abandonment of sexual aims, a desexualization—a kind of sublimation, therefore. Indeed the question arises, and deserves careful consideration, whether this is not the universal road to sublimation, whether all sublimation does not take place through the mediation of the ego, which begins by changing sexual object-libido into narcissistic libido and then perhaps goes on to give it another aim.

Internalization, then, can be described on the level of superego formation as transformation of an erotic object-choice (oedipal relations) into an alteration of the ego—that is, as transformation of object libido into narcissistic libido. This involves "desexualization"

---

imprecisions in terminology condoned in the absence of words that would be completely neutral relative to these differentiations and distinctions.

The imprecision of the term *narcissistic* is compounded by the fact that it has been used to refer to libido, or "interest," directed to the self or ego as a whole, as well as to refer to those libidinal processes that establish and maintain the very unity of that self. Both sources of confusion are indications of problems in rational language and in the psychology of the individual that are poorly understood.

in the sense that it is no longer the external object, whether "out there" or in fantasy, that is desired: The aim of satisfaction by means of an object is abandoned; the aim is changed. This Freud calls a *desexualization*, a kind of sublimation. But it must be remembered that narcissistic libido still is libido—not in the original narrow sense of sexual object-cathexis, but in the widened sense of the life or love instinct, of eros. Nothing shows Freud's meaning more clearly than his anthropomorphic simile: "When the ego assumes the features of the object, it is forcing itself, so to speak, upon the id as a love-object and is trying to make good the id's loss by saying: 'Look, you can love me too—I am so like the object' " (1923b, p. 30).

This is Freud's thought: the "ego as a whole" (the equivalent of Hartmann's *self*) is held together by libidinal, erotic bonds which in their basic nature are not different from those bonds obtaining in object relations. Indeed, narcissistic and object bonds—once they are differentiated as such—often remain intermingled, or intermingle again, and are strongly colored and influenced by one another; the two "scenes of action" are in more or less constant interplay.[3] In this view sublimation comes about by a change of object libido into narcissistic libido, by an internalizing transformation of passion or desire, by transformation of object relations into intrapsychic interactions— once the interpsychic and the intrapsychic are differentiated. The universal road to sublimation is, therefore, internalization. Through internalization the character of objects themselves and of object-relations changes. Likewise, the nature of objectives and pursuits in the outer world ("aims") changes and "substitutes" become available "through the mediation of the ego" in its interplay with the external scene of action. Objects, object relations, and objectives may be said to be reorganized or re-created through this reciprocal interplay. The essential part civilization and education play in sublimation, as well as

3. For Freud's discussion of internal narcissistic bonds see *Beyond the Pleasure Principle* (1920), especially pp. 50, 52. For his discussion of the development of and changes in his instinct theory, see pp. 52–55 and n. 1, pp. 60–61. My presentation is in no small measure based on these important texts.

the essential part sublimation and the mediation of the ego play in the emergence and advancement of civilization, should be seen in this light. Freud uses the phrase "desexualized Eros" (1923b, p. 44) to mean that the binding and uniting of eros is now internally displayed. He also means to say that, as this occurs, objects and aims in the external world change their character; they become, or are apt to become, "desexualized" themselves because they are imbued with a changed cathexis, one that is no longer unmodified object-libidinal cathexis.

The polarization that arises in the differentiation of primary narcissism into narcissistic and object libido is counterbalanced, modulated, tempered, by sublimation. Relations with external objects change into internal, "narcissistic" relations, and these desexualized libidinal bonds are instrumental in molding aims and relations with external objects, so that these themselves are likely to become desexualized. Freud said that the shadow of the object falls on the ego. Equally, the shadow of the altered ego falls on objects and object relations. Sublimation is a kind of reconciliation of the subject-object dichotomy—an atonement for that polarization (the word *atone* derives from *at one*) and a narrowing of the gulf between object libido and narcissistic libido, between object world and self.[4]

Hartmann, in his "Notes on the Theory of Sublimation" (1955), places the concepts of neutralization and neutralized energy at the center of his considerations. My proposition that sublimation represents a reconciliation in the sense indicated above is related to these "economic" concepts. But my approach is different from Hartmann's in important respects. Hartmann contrasts "the purely instinctual strivings" and their "mode of discharge" with the mode of energy in the ego (p. 24). I maintain that both narcissism and the structure of the ego resulting from the organization of narcissistic libido are in-

4. I have dealt with aspects of atonement, reconciliation, and guilt in "The Waning of the Oedipus Complex" ([1979] 1980, pp. 387–95) and shall return to these issues in a subsequent chapter.

stinctual in origin and nature, that narcissistic libido is no less instinctual than object libido. Freud relinquished the duality of sexual and ego instincts in favor of his unified and widened concept of libido in part to underscore the basic unity of sexuality and spirituality (see the Leonardo discussion in the previous chapter). The duality of life and death instincts, it should be emphasized again, is of a different order. If one operates with the concept of psychic energy, it is neither the nature of their energy nor its source that marks the difference between the ego and the id, but, rather, the way in which and the level at which energy is organized. To assume the existence of a neutral psychic energy which in the form of ego controls and influences instinctual energy is to reinstate an original dichotomy of ego and id. The delay of immediate instinctual discharge of which Hartmann speaks is not primarily due to "control by the ego," an ego that would have to have sources of energy of a different and autonomous kind from those of the id. (Hartmann acknowledges this in his term *primary autonomy of the ego*). Instead, this delay is the resultant of that organization of instinctual energy which we call by the name of ego.

I shall return to these problems when I discuss Winnicott's contributions. It is my intention not to eliminate the concept of neutralization from the discussion of sublimation but to give it a meaning richer than a strictly economic one and to free it from the implication that the energy involved here is noninstinctual or that it is controlled by a noninstinctual energy source. Greenacre (1957) and E. Kris (1955) have expressed misgivings about treating the term neutralization as equivalent to sublimation insofar as neutralization suggests something noninstinctual. As Freud said of Leonardo, passion is not absent in sublimation, and it is especially active and experienced in creative work, be it of a scientific, artistic, therapeutic, or religious nature, or of any other kind.

Narcissistic and object libido, identification and object cathexis, are products of differentiation within primary narcissism, that is, within the mother-infant matrix of psychic life. Sublimation, in this

21

view, involves an internal re-creative return toward that matrix,[5] a reconciliation of the polarized elements produced by individuation and, one may suspect, by sexual differentiation. Sublimation thus brings together what had become separate. It "plays a decisive part in the mastery of reality" (Hartmann 1955)—mastery conceived not as domination but as coming to terms—as it brings external and material reality within the compass of psychic reality, and psychic reality within the sweep of external reality. In its most developed form in creative work it culminates in celebration. This "manic" element of sublimation is not a denial, or not only that, but an affirmation of unity as well. Yet the organization of the ego itself, to the extent to which it is nonrepressive, is such celebration already.

I now turn to Winnicott's approach to sublimation, which is far closer to mine. He also starts from the mother-infant matrix. On the basis of his study "Transitional Objects and Transitional Phenomena" (1953), he goes on to examine what he calls "The Location of Cultural Experience," relating it to play (1967). In the latter paper he begins as follows:

> Freud did not have a place in his topography of the mind for the experience of things cultural. He gave new value to inner psychic reality, and from this came a new value for things that are actual and truly external. Freud used the word 'sublimation' to point the way to a place where cultural experience is meaningful, but perhaps he did not get so far as to tell us where in the mind cultural experience is. (P. 368)

He notes that "play is in fact neither a matter of inner psychic reality nor a matter of external reality." What he calls cultural experience belongs to the area of play or is an extension of that area. The transitional object, he says, "is a symbol of the union of the baby and

---

5. *Mother-infant matrix* must be understood as a shorthand expression: the matrix always "contains" the father, by virtue of his biological-psychological functions and significance, even, and perhaps most poignantly, as the absent one.

the mother." In this context "symbol" means that the transitional object is an embodiment of that union. Winnicott continues: "The use of an object symbolizes the union of two now separate things, baby and mother, *at the point of the initiation of their state of separateness*" (p. 369; Winnicott's italics). He speaks of a "separation that is not a separation but a form of union."

In "Transitional Objects and Transitional Phenomena" Winnicott writes, italicizing the passage: "Of the transitional object it can be said that it is a matter of agreement between us and the baby that we will never ask the question 'Did you conceive of this or was it presented to you from without?' The important point is that no decision on this point is expected. The question is not to be formulated" (p. 95). Later he writes:

> No human being is free from the strain of relating inner and outer reality, and . . . relief from this strain is provided by an intermediate area of experience which is not challenged (arts, religion, etc.). This intermediate area is in direct continuity with the play area of the small child who is 'lost' in play. . . . We do not challenge the infant in regard to subjectivity or objectivity just here where there is the transitional object. (P. 96)

Winnicott summarizes as follows: "This intermediate area of experience, unchallenged in respect of its belonging to inner or external (shared) reality, constitutes the greater part of the infant's experience and throughout life is retained in the intense experiencing that belongs to the arts and to religion and to imaginative living, and to creative scientific work" (p. 97).

Winnicott considers the area of cultural experience and of sublimation in light of his transitional phenomena, an example of which is the transitional object of the infant, representing a "separation that is not a separation but a form of union," and this "at the point of the initiation of their state of separateness." In referring to more advanced forms of sublimation, I have called this kind of union a reconciliation of polarities, of separateness. The point of initiation of a state of separateness can be defined as the "point" at which differentiation occurs. It is a unitary field that undergoes differentiation—in the case of the baby, it is the mother-infant psychic matrix; in the case of the older child and adult, a field represented by their embeddedness in the environmental world, from which they become alienated and which they alienate. In genuine sublimation this alienating differentiation is being reversed in such a way that a fresh unity is created by an act of uniting. In this reversal—a restoration of unity—there comes into being a *differentiated unity* (a manifold) that captures separateness in the act of uniting, and unity in the act of separating. I shall return to this aspect of transitional phenomena in a subsequent chapter on symbolism.

In "The Location of Cultural Experience," Winnicott writes that transitional phenomena "have no climax. This distinguishes them from phenomena that have instinctual backing, where the orgiastic element plays an essential part, and where satisfactions are closely linked with climax. Here comes in Hartmann's concept of neutralization. But these [transitional] phenomena . . . belong to the *experience of relating to objects*" (1967, p. 369; Winnicott's italics). His climactic phenomena that have "instinctual backing" can be roughly correlated with object cathexis, and the nonclimactic ones with narcissistic cathexis. I believe that Winnicott's distinction between nonclimactic and climactic phenomena is important for our understanding of sublimatory processes, although one might ask whether the culmination in celebration—the "manic" element I alluded to—might not be a form of climactic phenomena. Winnicott seems to fall back on the old concept of libido in which the term is equated with and restricted to object libido and the discharge satisfactions specific to it.

Winnicott stresses that the nonclimactic phenomena belong to the experience of relating to objects. If we agree that these phenomena and experiences are not challengeable in respect to subjectivity or objectivity—that, concerning them, the question "subjective or objective?" is not to be formulated—then "relating to objects" here refers to the kind of relatedness that Kohut tried to capture with the term *selfobject*. Winnicott suggests that this relatedness is comparable to the kind of "electricity" that, he says, "seems to generate in meaningful or intimate contact, and that is a feature when two people are in love" (1967, p. 369). It is like waves, oscillations, vibrations in a magnetic field, not like a discharge phenomenon. Winnicott attributes this feature to "phenomena of the play area [having] infinite variability" as compared to the relative stereotypy of discharge phenomena (pp. 369–70). His invoking Hartmann's term *neutralization* here might then suggest a neutrality that does not allow the question "subject or object?" to be formulated (*neuter* derives from *ne uter*, "not either"). But this neutrality also suggests the absence of discharge. This second aspect of neutrality leads us to the issues of instinctual aim, aim inhibition, and the nature of satisfaction.

Aim inhibition is a central feature in the classical theory of sublimation. Freud had what Winnicott calls nonclimactic phenomena in mind when he spoke of tender-affectionate, "aim-inhibited" currents. These Freud subsumed under sublimation, particularly because of the factor of aim inhibition. I suggest that the distinction between "tender" and "sexual" impulsions is akin to the distinctions between identification and object cathexis, between narcissistic libido and object libido, and between self and object world. All these distinctions are based on, and worded in terms of relatively advanced stages of psychic development. In his postscript to *Group Psychology and the Analysis of the Ego* (1921), Freud discusses the distinction between direct and aim-inhibited sexual instincts and is quite clear about his conviction that tender-affectionate currents are secondary to direct sexual impulses, that these strivings have been diverted from their original sexual aims. But he also speaks of the "first formation of infantile love", which belongs to the Oedipus complex, and of the subsequent or concomitant appearance of tender strivings and emotional bonds. In an interesting passage he writes: "All the feelings that

25

the child experiences for his parents and caretakers continue without barrier into the wishes that give expression to the child's sexual strivings. The child demands from these loved ones all the tendernesses known to him." Freud speaks here of the child's wanting to kiss, to touch, to look at them and at their genitals, of his promising to marry Mother, and so forth. There is a confluence, he writes, of tender, jealous feelings and sexual intentions. A chord is struck here that does not quite resonate with Freud's assertion that tender-affectionate currents develop out of strivings that have a "sexual aim" through diversion from this sexual aim. Perhaps he betrays his uneasiness when he writes, "There is some difficulty in giving a description of such a diversion of aim that will conform to the requirements of metapsychology" (1921, pp. 137, 138).[6]

In "Instincts and Their Vicissitudes" (1915a), Freud gives the following definition of an instinctual aim: "The aim of an instinct is in every instance satisfaction, which can only be obtained by removing the state of stimulation at the source of the instinct" (p. 122). Under this equation of satisfaction with removal of stimulation, that is, with discharge of tension (*Abfuhr*), climactic phenomena constitute the prototype for satisfaction. Freud goes on to describe how, while the final aim (*Endziel*) of an instinct remains unchangeable, intermediate aims may arise. He adds that there are processes that go for a while in the direction of satisfaction but then undergo an inhibition or diversion—the aim-inhibited instincts.

Freud's conception of instinctual aim—satisfaction by discharge of instinctual tension—categorizes nonclimactic phenomena, or

6. Compare G. W. 13: 154, 155. I have given my own translation of the quotation starting with "All the feelings that the child experiences . . .", in the belief that it is more faithful to Freud's text than is Strachey's translation. In particular, the words "continue without barrier into the wishes" (*setzen sich ohne Schranke in die Wuensche fort*) should be preserved as they evoke the absence of the incest barrier in the first formation of the child's love life and the nondifferentiation of what are becoming two different currents. It should be stressed again that, as is clear from later passages of the postscript, Freud is mainly concerned here with oedipal and especially with post-oedipal development, not with the preoedipal antecedents of love life.

processes in which discharge phenomena are not an essential element, *by definition* as aim-inhibited or as having diverted or intermediate aims. If nonclimactic phenomena are to have a status of their own, as opposed to being derived from discharge processes, then the definition requires that they not be instinctual. Here, it seems, is the origin of the idea that "the ego" disposes of energies that are noninstinctual (the primary autonomy of the ego). As mentioned before, Freud's statement that it is difficult to give a metapsychological description of aim diversion and inhibition may well indicate his awareness that ultimately his concepts of primary narcissism and narcissistic libido do not conform well with the object libido–derived definition of instinctual aim. One must consider that "satisfaction" (Freud's term is *Befriedigung*, from *befriedigen*—literally, "to appease, pacify") may be achieved by means other than elimination (or reduction) of a state of tension or stimulation. If there is such a thing as a life instinct, its "aim" would be satisfaction through the attainment of higher, more differentiated unities, in which tension is not eliminated but "bound"—satisfaction of a different kind. Only if it is assumed that *constancy* is achieved solely in a state of rest, of nonexcitation (the constancy, or unpleasure, principle), only then is the ultimate aim of an instinct "in every instance" satisfaction by "climax."

In "The Economic Problem of Masochism," published almost ten years after "Instincts and Their Vicissitudes", Freud comes to different conclusions:

> Pleasure and unpleasure . . . cannot be referred to an increase or decrease of a quantity (which we describe as 'tension due to stimulus'), although they obviously have a great deal to do with that factor. It appears that they depend, not on this quantitative factor, but on some characteristic of it which we can only describe as a qualitative one. If we were able to say what this qualitative characteristic is, we should be much further advanced in psychology. Perhaps it is the rhythm, the temporal sequence of changes, rises and falls in the quantity of stimulus. We do not know. (1924a, pp. 159–60)

He distinguishes in that paper between the constancy principle—or, as he calls it here, the Nirvana principle—and the pleasure-unpleasure principle. It is worthwhile to quote in full the steps he takes in arriving at this new distinction:

> We have unhesitatingly identified the pleasure-unpleasure principle with this Nirvana principle. Every unpleasure ought thus to coincide with a heightening, and every pleasure with a lowering, of mental tension due to stimulus; the Nirvana principle (and the pleasure principle which is supposedly identical with it) would be entirely in the service of the death instincts, whose aim is to conduct the restlessness of life into the stability of the inorganic state, and it would have the function of giving warnings against the demands of the life instincts— the libido—which try to disturb the intended course of life. But such a view cannot be correct. It seems that in the series of feelings of tension we have a direct sense of the increase and decrease of the amounts of stimulus, and it cannot be doubted that there are pleasurable tensions and unpleasurable relaxations of tension. (1924a, pp. 159–60)[7]

Freud then posits three different *aims*, which may variously combine, overlap, or conflict with each other; they correspond to the three principles involved—namely, the Nirvana principle, the pleasure principle (note that the pleasure principle is no longer identical with the Nirvana principle), and the reality principle. The aims are described as follows: "in one case [Nirvana principle] a quantitative reduction of the stimulus-load, in another [pleasure principle] a qualitative characteristic of it, and lastly [reality principle] a temporal deferment of the discharge of the stimulus and a temporary acquiescence in the unpleasure of tension" (ibid., p. 161).[8] The last aim, under the rule of the reality principle, which represents the influence of the external world, would show what Freud calls aim inhibition

7. By "a direct sense of the increase and decrease of the amounts of stimulus" Freud means, I suppose, that one may sense variations in quantity (*Reizgroesse*) by means that are not dependent on experiencing discomfort or comfort.

8. G. W. 13:373 (my own translation; Strachey's is not precise).

28

(or diversion). The outstanding example of the aim that is "a qualitative characteristic of the stimulation-load" is the pleasure experienced in the increase of sexual excitation (Freud clearly has in mind object-libidinal tension). But, as he says, "it clearly is not the only one" (1924a, p. 160).

Thus by 1924 Freud no longer assumed that the aim of an instinct is in every instance satisfaction *by removal of stimulation*. Furthermore, the assumption that sublimation is characterized by the inhibition of that particular aim becomes at least doubtful. It also may be questioned now whether the operation of the reality principle inevitably means that the aim of stimulus removal is inhibited. The reality principle, as a modification of the *revised* pleasure principle, may be in the service of the second-named aim, attainment of "a qualitative characteristic of the stimulus-load." If the reality principle is no longer understood as simply a modification of the Nirvana or old pleasure-unpleasure principle but is understood as a modification of the new pleasure principle and the demands of the libido, or life instinct, as well (p. 160), then "reality", the influence of the external world, might operate quite differently, not only leading to deferment or inhibition of stimulus discharge. The external world could be a factor in creating the qualitative characteristic of the stimulus load which would not primarily have to do with discharge inhibition. Here Freud's concept of *hypercathexis* through the linking of "thing presentations" and "word presentations" (1915, pp. 201–02) is relevant. In a previous paper (Loewald [1978] 1980, especially pp. 181ff.). I have pointed out that in such hypercathexis by the linkage of word presentations with the corresponding thing presentations, words are originally provided by the human environment to the infant—that is, by a specific element, a specific influence, of the external world. It should not be overlooked that this is the root phenomenon of what in psychoanalysis is called *interpretation*. Hypercathexis, as Freud points out in "The Unconscious" (1915b), may lead to higher psychic organization and thereby to a change in the quality of the stimulus load.

My contention is that we are led astray by Freud's assertion (1924a, p. 161) that in the case of the reality principle the aim is a deferment of stimulus discharge and an acquiescence in the unpleasure of tension; that in this formulation he reverts unwittingly to the conceptions, just relinquished, of pleasure as the reduction or absence of tension and of the reality principle as a modification of the old unpleasure principle brought about by the influence of external reality. I cannot emphasize enough that it was the introduction of the idea of the life instinct (which encompassed different conceptions of pleasure and of the pleasure principle) that was a true and unsettling innovation in psychoanalytic theory—an innovation that Freud could no longer circumvent but with which he felt much less at home than he did with the death instinct (for a summary of Freud's view on life and death instincts as of 1923, see 1923, pp. 258–59).

Winnicott's phenomena that have no climax appear to show an "aim" that consists in a qualitative characteristic of the stimulation load. One may perhaps speak of neutralization if this is meant to imply not that a decrease of tension is involved or that the processes involved are noninstinctual, but that an organization of excitation is taking place in which discharge is not an essential element in the attainment of pleasure. This may occur in the pleasure of heightened sexual excitement (acknowledging that anticipation of climax is often important here), in the pleasure of the nonclimactic intimacy of being in love, or in that binding of tension involved in higher psychic organization. The endopsychic binding of excitation can be seen as an equivalent of those nonclimactic phenomena that Winnicott describes as belonging to the experience of relating to objects but which, as we have seen, must not be challenged—also according to Winnicott—by the question "subject or object?" The ultimate aim of such binding of tension is not satisfaction in the form of removal of the state of stimulation by discharge on or through an object (see Freud 1915a, p. 122). Is it perpetuation of tension, of the excitation inherent in living substance? One may speculate (and recent theories

30

of physical science point in that direction) that inorganic matter and its constituent molecules, atoms, and so on, manifest a relatively permanent phase or form of bound energy. The appropriate description would be *relatively* permanent because it would pertain on a time scale far beyond the ordinary human one. The state of rest to which the constancy or unpleasure principle refers would not be absolute but relative, would be, on a cosmic and atomic time scale, "life."[9] Also, in individual instinctual life the aim of perpetuation of tension by transindividual and endopsychic binding would fit better with the human wish for immortality than does the single aim of death and a complete state of rest.

In sum, this position postulates the existence of instinctual processes that do not press for discharge,[10] of pleasures and satisfactions not linked to discharge or diminution of excitation, and of unpleasure linked not to increase of excitation but to lowering of tension. Furthermore, there appears to be unpleasure connected with a qualitative change, a change in the organization of instinctual processes in the direction of lower levels of organization (which, it is true, may entail increased tension).

9. In "An Outline of Psycho-Analysis" Freud writes: "If we assume that living things came later than inanimate ones and arose from them, then the death instinct fits in with the formula we have proposed to the effect that instincts tend towards a return to an earlier state. In the case of Eros (or the love instinct) we cannot apply this formula. To do so would presuppose that living substance was once a unity which had later been torn apart and was now striving towards re-union" (1940, pp. 148–49). See also the passage in "Analysis Terminable and Interminable" referring to Empedocles' "cosmic phantasy" concerning the two principles—love and strife—that govern "events in the life of the universe and in the life of the mind" (Freud 1937, pp. 245–47). Again in the "Outline" Freud writes: "The analogy of our two basic instincts extends from the sphere of living things to the pair of opposing forces—attraction and repulsion—which rule in the inorganic world." And, in a footnote, he refers once more to Empedocles (1940, p. 149).

10. It is, of course, unquestionable that pressure [*Drang*], exercising pressure [*Draengen*], is a characteristic of all instincts—"in fact," Freud said, "their very essence. Every instinct is a piece of activity" (1915a, p. 122). But that is different from saying that it is pressure toward discharge and a state of rest.

We are far from adequately understanding the pleasure in higher organization and the unpleasure in less or lower organization. Part of the difficulty seems to be the fact that theorists in this area are preoccupied with quantitative factors and consequently neglect phenomena of *resonance* in favor of data on input and output of energy quanta. "Stimulation" should not be conceived exclusively as increase of the quantity of excitation; in many instances it can be thought of as resonance with the "wave length" of a neighboring system. Stimulation can result from an openness to the latter's level of binding or organization of activity. The neighboring system, in the case of such hypercathexis is simultaneously open to, in tune with, the "receiving" system. Stimulation, in such resonance, would consist in qualitative change of some kind: the organization of the degree of tension preexisting in the receiving system is changed. As Freud said of the qualitative characteristic in pleasure and unpleasure, so is resonance a phenomenon implicated with rhythm, with time, in ways that are not clear. But it is not likely that the idea of "rises and falls in the quantity of stimulus" will help our understanding.

For the sake of clarity, let me recapitulate two important departures from classical psychoanalytic theory contained in the foregoing considerations:

1. The first given to be assumed in psychoanalytic psychology is an interactional field, represented in its most primitive form by the infant-mother psychic matrix. What we call *instincts* in psychoanalysis—libido-aggression, or erotic-destructive, or life and death instincts—do not *ab initio* reside in an already separate psychic unit, the infant (or infant-self). In reference to the earliest stages of development, *instinct* (or *instinctual drive*) is a term for (interactional) psychic processes occurring in that matrix. Over the course of psychic differentiation—individuation—instincts become the motivational forces of an internal repertoire of the infant. The repertoire is by its origins already marked by contributions from the motivational repertoire of the caretakers; it is not the

manifestation of an innately autonomous infantile psyche. Recent work by analysts of children and by researchers in the growing field of "infant psychiatry" is consistent, in my view, with such a proposition. *Primary narcissism* then is a title for the instinctual life of the mother-infant matrix. *Libido*—the psychoanalytic term for the erotic or sexual aspect of instinct—and aggression (although the aspect of aggression requires separate considerations) are at first undifferentiated from each other and nondifferentiating as to "object" and "self." The terms *object libido* and *narcissistic libido* conceptualize the differentiations taking place in the libidinal currents of primary narcissism. At the primary narcissistic stage it makes no sense—to use Winnicott's expression—to challenge libido with these alternatives. I shall later discuss the idea—implicit in Winnicott's views on the location of cultural experience—that this "stage," rather than becoming extinct or being relinquished in the course of individuation, remains an active ingredient or constitutive element in individual experience, although the level of complexity and organization of the adult's psychic matrix in which it is embedded is vastly different.

2. Sublimation is not a form of defense—not even of "successful" defense—against instinctual life, the id, desire, passion, the unconscious; instead sublimation belongs in the area of ego development and of internalization as distinguished from defense. I conceptualize its dynamic quality broadly as *reconciliation*.

EXCURSUS ON BIOLOGICAL AND PSYCHOANALYTIC DISCOURSE

Here and elsewhere, I have stressed that I use *instinct* as a psychoanalytic and not as a biological-physiological (or ethological) concept. This tends to be misconstrued as implying that for me instinct (*Trieb*) is unrelated to the body, the organism—that I thus disregard Freud's steadfast injunction that his instinct concept is a borderland concept, on the border between what we conceive of as the somatic and the psychic realms. Freud has wavered between characterizing instinct as an organic stimulus—a "need" affecting the psychic apparatus—and as a psychic representative of such an organic need-stimulus. Speaking within the framework of these Freudian theoretical formulations, I have opted for conceptualizing instinct as a psychic representative of organic needs and not as itself an organic stimulus operating on the psyche—despite my serious misgivings concerning the obscurities and ambiguities of the terms *representative* and *representation*. The word *representative* suggests or implies a discourse which is on a plane different from the plane of discourse implied when speaking of that which is represented by the representative. The term *representation* points to a relatedness between two or more entities which is not that of cause and effect (for example, organic stimulus as cause, psychic process as effect). If, however, *Trieb* is thought of as a somatic sitmulus on the psyche, a cause-effect relationship between soma and psyche is postulated, whereas *soma* and *psyche*—superficial appearances notwithstanding—signify not two different items of reality but two different modes of experiencing or ordering reality. Hence we frequently use and think of these terms simultaneously or somehow intermingle them; this is less objectionable than is the implication of cause-effect relation between them or, for that matter, than is regarding one as more real or more true than the other. As long as one remains within the framework of modern natural science—and thedistinction between maternal reality and psychic reality is bound to that framework—all one can say is that the biological is a realm different from the psychological insofar as the selfsame material of experience is ordered and integrated differently in each. Psychoanalysis, its self-understanding limited by that framework, has opted for regarding its material of experience as "psychic," while remaining cognizant of, and in communication with, the biological perspective. As psychoanalysts committed to the tradition of modern science, we integrate our experience as psychic, not in the form of what we call physical reality.

I question this commitment with all its implications, but for the time being it remains a—somewhat shaken—fact of intellectual life. [11]

11. I have drawn attention to and elaborated on these issues in chapter three of my paper "On Motivation and Instinct Theory" ([1972] 1980, pp. 124–26). The reader is referred to that source for a fuller understanding of the problems involved.

CHAPTER THREE

The Traditional Theory of Sublimation

and Defense

In the preceding chapter I discussed sublimation theory mainly from a perspective that became apparent with the introduction into psychoanalytic theory of the concepts of narcissism and internalization. Freud articulated these ideas comparatively late in the development of his new science. The chief experiential basis for this critical change seems to have been his growing interest in ego formation and development, in infantile and primitive mentality and psychotic pathology, and in problems connected with the phenomena of aggression and guilt. I have described how and why his instinct theory changed, with the result that the concepts of sexuality, libido, and eros, as well as of aggression and the destructive instinct, were applied now to a much wider range of phenomena than previously.

There are features of sublimation, nevertheless, that are best discussed in conjunction with the issue of defense mechanisms and in the light of, as one might say, the psychoanalytic common-sense view of libido as object libido. I came to the conclusion that sublimation cannot be subsumed under the general heading of defense (which is not to deny that identificatory processes may be, and often are, in the service of defense). For the most part, however, owing predominantly to traditional theoretical preconceptions, sublimation *has* been viewed as defense—albeit "successful" defense—and a comparison with genuine basic defenses will be illuminating. In what follows, the term *instinctual* will refer—in accordance with prenarcissism theory—to object libido and to aggression in relation to objects.

In contrast to what is the case in repression, in sublimation instinctual impulses are said not to be averted, but to be diverted from their aim of satisfaction in immediate discharge. Their corresponding percepts, memories, and fantasies are not repressed (as occurs in countercathexis) but instead, according to this viewpoint, are made more acceptable by some disguise or embellishment. The diversion of impulse is described as delay or aim inhibition, possibly leading to a substitute aim. Freud spoke of a "laxity" or easy reversibility of repression that makes sublimation possible. It is instructive to see how he compared the two when speaking to a general academic audience. The occasion was one of the lectures on psychoanalysis he gave at Clark University in Worcester, Massachusetts.

[One] outcome of the work of psycho-analysis is that it then becomes possible for the unconscious instincts revealed by it to be employed for the useful purposes which they would have found earlier if development had not been interrupted [by repression]. For the extirpation of the infantile wishful impulses is by no means the ideal aim of development. Owing to their repression, neurotics have sacrificed many sources of mental energy whose contributions would have been of great value in the formation of their character and in their activity in life. We know a far more expedient process of development, called 'sublimation', in which the energy of the infantile wishful impulses is not cut off but remains ready for use—the unserviceable aim of the various impulses being replaced by one that is higher, and perhaps no longer sexual. It happens to be precisely the components of the *sexual* instinct that are specially marked by a capacity of this kind for sublimation, for exchanging their sexual aim for another one which is comparatively remote and socially valuable. It is probable that we owe our highest cultural successes to the contributions of energy made in this

37

way to our mental functions. Premature repression makes the sublimation of the repressed instinct impossible; when the repression is lifted,
the path to sublimation becomes free once more. (1910a pp. 53–54;
Freud's italics)

Sublimation, again unlike repression, is described here not as anti-
instinctual but as utilizing, as it were, instinctual forces for particular
acceptable or highly valued purposes through channeling and modu-
lating them. Repression, being anti-instinctual, prevents sublimation, whereas the removal of repression facilitates it. It is as if in true
sublimation the vital power of passion shines through in the very
perfection of mastery. In terminology of a later period: Whereas
repression means exclusion of instinctual currents from the coherent
ego, and thus restriction or impoverishment of the ego; in sublimation these currents are encompassed within the ego-organization by
way of channeling, organizing processes.

In the preceding paragraph I spoke of "true" sublimation, in contradistinction to sublimation which is not genuine or is flawed in
some way (see chap. 1). Freud alludes to this issue in one of his
papers on technique. He also makes several other observations which
it is important to keep in mind:

> A . . . temptation arises out of the educative activity which, in psycho-
> analytic treatment, devolves on the doctor without any deliberate
> intention on his part. When the developmental inhibitions are re-
> solved, it happens of itself that the doctor finds himself in a position to
> indicate new aims for the trends that have been liberated. It is then no
> more than a natural ambition if he endeavours to make something
> specially excellent of a person whom he has been at such pains to free
> from his neurosis and if he prescribes high aims for his wishes. But
> here . . . the doctor should hold himself in check, and take the pa-
> tient's capacities (*Eignung*, aptitude) rather than his own desires as
> guide. Not every neurotic has a high talent for sublimation; one can
> assume of many of them that they would not have fallen ill at all if
> they had possessed the art of sublimating their instincts. If we press

them unduly towards sublimation and cut them off from the most accessible and convenient instinctual satisfactions, we shall usually make life even harder for them than they feel it in any case. As a doctor, one must above all be tolerant to the weakness of a patient, and must be content if one has won back some degree of capacity for work and enjoyment for a person even of only moderate worth. . . . It must further be borne in mind that many people fall ill precisely from an attempt to sublimate their instincts beyond the degree permitted by their organization and that in those who have a capacity for sublimation the process usually takes place of itself as soon as their inhibitions have been overcome by analysis. (1912a, pp. 118–19)

In the last sentence of this passage Freud alludes to pseudosublimation, suggesting that such artificial sublimation has its own pathogenic effects. Freud distinguishes between two kinds of educative activity involved in psychoanalytic treatment: One is implicit in the fact that the analyst aims at resolutions of developmental inhibitions (*Entwicklungshemmungen*), but the effect of this liberating activity of the analyst is to put him in a position to indicate new aims for the instinctual trends present in his patient. The latter is a more formal, more directive kind of education; Freud does not reject it, but he recommends that it be used with great caution and restraint so as to adapt to the patient's disposition and aptitude for sublimation. If the analyst is to be a civilizing agent, in the best sense of the word *civilizing,* then in *forcefully* directing the patient to higher aims he undoes his own work and contributes to further misery and "discontent" instead of promoting the patient's own development. The term *sublimation* here is confined to the narrower sense of higher cultural development rather than carrying the more basic and comprehensive sense in which ego development itself is understood as a sublimatory process. When specific higher cultural values are emphasized, sublimation begins to be seen as a talent or an "art" possessed only by a fortunate minority.

In contrast to his view of repression, Freud described the defense

39

mechanism of reaction formation as a kind of sublimation, especially in regard to character formation (see the discussion of Fenichel in the Introduction). Cleanliness and orderliness, for instance, are traits that master anal impulses in the service of ego organization. In clinical work it is our assessment of the flexibility and adaptiveness of such traits that decides to a large extent whether we consider them in terms of reaction formation (as we do if they are inflexible and all-pervasive) or of sublimation. But the borders between normal character traits and character neurosis are fluid. The issue of the *value* of the direction and outcome of such psychic processes enters here: the adaptive value and the range of a character trait seem to determine our view one way or the other. In theoretical terms, one would say that reaction formation involves opposition to, countercathexis against, the relevant instinctual currents—and thus is a form of disavowing them or turning them into their opposite—while sublimation does not. Much analytic work is concerned with redressing an economic imbalance, that is, to tip the scales in favor of optimally utilizing instinctual impulses versus fighting against them. Intellectualization, with its two faces of defense and of advance and expansion in mental life (as described particularly by Anna Freud [1946, pp. 172–80]), furnishes a good example of the fluctuations between reaction formation and sublimation.

Here the well-known question comes to mind: What does the loosening or removing of repressions and other defenses do to traits and activities, such as artistic or scientific abilities and pursuits, that are in the realm of sublimation? Under favorable circumstances, far from undoing or unraveling sublimations, it makes formerly blocked, more widely ranging instinctual energy available for such work. This can be observed particularly in the analytic work, when the loosening of obsessive-compulsive defenses, for example, allows libidinal-aggressive currents toward the analyst in the transference to be used for the analytic work itself and for ego expansion. In many instances, however, valid sublimations are protected and supported by certain defensive barriers against instinctual impulses that threaten them. One should note that the degree of elasticity of the defenses determines whether they protect or hinder sublimation. Thus sublimations may become quite vulnerable or, at least temporarily, undone, if deprived of protective defenses.

The fact that psychic processes and states in vivo are always fluid and complex should not prevent us from making conceptual distinctions. While reaction formation implies the factor of a countervailing force that reacts against and opposes the original impulse, sublimation implies a concurrent, coordinate factor, a form of *hypercathexis* instead of countercathexis. This kind of hypercathexis does not increase the intensity of the impulse but, rather, heightens its level and range of organization. (I again refer here to the concept of hypercathexis as Freud used it in "The Unconscious" [1915b] when discussing the formation of secondary process and of the preconscious. In chapter 2 I linked hypercathexis with resonance, as contrasted with increase in the amount or quantity of stimulation.) The concurrent no less than the opposing factor is related to the caretaking environment. Freud alluded to this as early as 1897: ["Phantasies] are made up from things that are *heard*, and made use of *subsequently*; thus they combine things that have been experienced and things that have been heard, past events (from the history of parents and ancestors) and things that have been seen by oneself" (Freud 1892–99, "Draft L" p. 248; Freud's italics).

To recapitulate the difference between repression (often seen as the prototype of defense) and sublimation: in the period before the narcissism theory of sublimation and prior to the emergence of the structural theory (id-ego-superego), and to some extent even in Freud's later work, sublimation is categorized as defense. Repression is a mechanism of defense by which the ego keeps itself relatively free of tension and conflict; it excludes disturbing instinctual impulses and their proximate derivatives by means of keeping them, or rendering them, unconscious. Sublimation is seen as another method of defense instigated by the ego: in sublimation instinctual impulses are diverted from their aim of direct discharge by inhibitory, deflecting delays that establish substitute and intermediate gratifications or utilize already established ones. The fundamental aim of satisfaction by discharge (according to the original pleasure-unpleasure principle) is not given up or blocked. Instead it is made more remote, due to the detours established by channeling, "binding", of instinctual impulses. The detours gain a provisional valid status of their own).[1] Sublimation is seen as a defensive, successful compromise. But repressed impulses, although repudiated or blocked by the ego, tend not to disappear altogether for long. Rather, they find substitute gratifications and expressions, too, in compromise formations such as dreams and symptoms (the "return of the repressed"). What is the difference between these formations and sublimations? Here we must have recourse to the idea that an essential ingredient in sublimation is the higher value of certain aims and objects, including the value of the ego itself as a higher form of psychic organization and human development. Higher values and purposes are not similarly attributed to dreams and symptoms. We also are reminded that the formation of an ego—as distinguished from an id—can be described as a sublimatory process and that a distinction between sublimation and ego formation is not easily made (see Introduction). This makes it difficult simply to say, with Fenichel, that in sublimation aim or object, or both, are changed "under the influence of the ego" (Fenichel 1945, p. 141).

The attribution of higher value to sublimations would be a manifestation of illusions shared by the human race, or by particular civilizations—illusions which are themselves defensive formations erected to cover, or to screen from consciousness, the stark reality of the instincts and of the frustrating external obstacles to their direct satisfaction. Once the ultimate governance of the unpleasure principle is granted, such a conception of sublimation has its own internal logic. In sublimatory activities one does sometimes experience a

---

1. For further discussion of the concept of defense and of the status of these "detours" see my paper "On Internalization" ([1973] 1980), especially pp. 71–72 and 73–80.

sense of the loss or absence of that vibrantly physical pleasure, that vital intensity and poignancy of living, that we feel when instinctual urges, sensual aims, and gratifying object are in unison. It also cannot be denied that much of our vaunting of sublimatory activities and achievements, of our exaltation of cultural values, has elements of self-deceit and hypocrisy, the freshness and immediacy of bodily pleasure being like the proverbial sour grapes. This is what made Freud so wary of high moral and cultural aspirations and values. At the same time he could not help but affirm the validity and power of sublimation as a means of coping with the unpalatable or intolerable exigencies of life (*Not des Lebens*) and of promoting civilized living. When all is said and done, he seemed to say, this is all we can hold on to. For Freud, science, itself admittedly a sublimatory activity and perhaps ultimately another mythology, was nonetheless the most mature way eliminating illusions and embellishments, to look at whatever reality may be with clear, unflinching eyes and to master reality in some measure. Science for him was an attempt at sober disillusionment, at that disenchantment he thought was necessary to attain true maturity. In the scientific work of psychoanalysis, sublimation turns around upon itself, and as it were against itself—to unmask itself.

Values and higher aims are not easily dispensed with as defining characteristics of sublimation, regardless of how strongly we declare ourselves committed to excluding value judgments from a scientific psychology. As soon as we think in terms of "higher" development and establish the life of the psyche as a privileged realm of existence, we introduce or yield to a valuation. If sublimations are based on shared illusions, as psychosocial beings we are at their mercy. "One thing only do I know for certain and that is that man's judgments of value follow directly his wishes for happiness—that, accordingly, they are an attempt to support his illusions with arguments." Freud wrote these lines after having repudiated any "intention to express an opinion upon the value of human civilization" (1930, penultimate and last page [pp. 144 and 145] *Civilization and Its Discontents*).

Before closing this chapter I wish to call attention to a factor in sublimation that Freud considered in the context of his distinction between sexual instinct and self-preservative, or ego-, instincts. This is the "leaning" of the sexual instincts on the satisfaction of the self-preservative instincts, which is markedly apparent in early phases of psychosexual development and continues in later phases, only gradually lessening as the sexual instincts become more or even fully independent (see "On Narcissism," 1914, p. 87). In English translation this dependence is called *anaclitic*, referring to the instincts themselves, not to the attachment of the child to the mother or to other caretakers. It is in "Instincts and Their Vicissitudes" that Freud connects this leaning specifically with sublimation:

> A portion of them [that is, of the sexual instincts] remains associated with the ego-instincts throughout life and furnishes them with libidinal components. . . . They are distinguished by possessing the capacity to act vicariously for one another to a wide extent and by being able to change their objects readily. In consequence of the latter properties they are capable of functions which are far removed from their original purposive actions [*Zielhandlungen*]—capable, that is, of sublimation. (1915a, p. 126)

In the light of our discussion of primary narcissism and the original inseparability of what later can be distinguished as ego libido and object libido, I would modify this statement of Freud's by saying that initially instinctual life is not dichotomous. And further, after bifurcation has taken place these two branches remain throughout life linked like companions to each other (in the above quotation the German *gesellt* is translated as "associated"). What is called the influence of the ego in sublimation exists because of the original unity of ego libido and object libido.

CHAPTER FOUR

Symbolism

*E*arlier, in connection with a passage from Freud's *Leonardo* paper (quoted on p. 10 above), I spoke of the idea that there are unitary experiences which give way to experiences of differentiation, but that in sublimation the experience of unity is restored, or at least evoked, in the form of symbolic linkage. A more extensive discussion of symbolism is now in order. The problem of illusion will be considered in this context.

Symbolization may be described as an imaginative act: Two different items of experience are linked in the mind in such a way that one represents the other. This representational relationship is distinguished from other kinds of relatedness, such as spatial, temporal, causal, or logical connection. These other forms of relatedness in turn may or may not influence or occasion the awareness or establishment of a symbolic relationship. Similarity seems to lend itself particularly well to symbolization, but one thing resembling another does not in and by itself make it a symbol of the other. The nonsymbolic relationships I mentioned impress us as being given by nature, as it were. A symbolic relationship, by contrast, impresses us as one in which we have a hand—not necessarily in the immediate sense, but certainly insofar as we are members of a cultural group or of the human race. A symbol seems, in a special way, always to be a symbol *for us*. Objects, events, processes, and activities, as well as the nonsymbolic relations between all of these, are perceived as phenomena existing in material or psychic reality—as autonomous facts, events, or relations. A part of the concept *symbol*, on the other hand, is the implication that an item extant in reality becomes a symbol only when our imagination casts it to represent or stand for something else that it is not. Perhaps our imagination connects two different items in this particular way on the basis of an obscure ancient or lost unity of experience. Anything having some form of circumscribed psychic or material existence can represent for us something else. This representational relatedness is not "objective" in the way in which, for example, one event is perceived as related to the next in objective time; it is "subjective" in the sense that we are aware that human imagination establishes, or has established in the past, the representational link between the symbol and the symbolized—a link that often gives the impression of an imaginative leap.

I should make the further preliminary remark that throughout this discussion, symbols are distinguished from signs and signals and from iconic and imitative portrayals. As defined here, signs bring to mind something that they point to, indicate, or recall (for instance, fever is a sign of illness; wet pavement is a sign of rain). Signals call attention to something else or give notice of it, often cueing some action or announcing some future event. Through a mental act that institutes symbolization, signs and signals may come to *represent* what hitherto they only pointed to or gave notice of: they, like the relationships mentioned before, may be pressed into service for symbolization.

Although much has been written about symbolism and symbol formation, it has received comparatively little attention from psychoanalysts. Among recent contributions from psychologists those of Piaget (1945) and especially of Werner and Kaplan (1963) stand out. I owe a great deal to Werner and Kaplan's book on symbol formation. Apart from early work by Freud, Jung, Stekel, Silberer, Sachs and Rank, and Jones, in my opinion the most valuable psychoanalytic discussions on problems of symbolism have come from the Melanie Klein school and from British authors influenced by her. Ernest Jones's 1916 paper was perhaps the one extensive attempt at a systematic approach to a psychoanalytic theory of symbolism (see

Jones 1948). It was published, of course, prior to the work of Melanie Klein and prior to the development of the theory of narcissism and the structural theory. Jones proposed and adhered to a very restrictive psychoanalytic concept of symbolism in that paper, to the discussion of which I shall return. I have not been able to study the vast general literature on symbolism with its many important contributions from disciplines such as philosophy, anthropology, aesthetics, linguistics, and literary criticism, nor do I refer, except very selectively, to the psychological and psychoanalytic literature on the subject. In the interest of presenting my own line of inquiry the scope of this chapter is quite limited. Nevertheless, my approach is clearly in the force field of the observations and the thought of many authors who have investigated problems of symbolism. I do not aim to be comprehensive or systematic, but instead deal with the subject from only a few angles.

I begin with one example of symbolization. In writing down (or voicing) my thoughts I give them visibility (or sound) in the form of symbols. Through my sensory-motor acts of writing, and reading what I wrote, the flow of my thinking acquires a materiality, a presence it did not have before. The words and sentences I write and see before me represent my thoughts in the form of visible symbols. Thus, these thoughts—immaterial insofar as I cannot apprehend them with my senses—materialize for me, and in materializing they gain distance from me and become elements of the world around me. They are "communicated" to me myself by these sensory-motor acts and can be communicated to others. I do not invent or construct material signs for my thoughts de novo, as I do when I draw a short line and decree that it shall signify the idea "horse." Words and sentences are embedded in a linguistic tradition of which I partake and which I share with others. They seem to derive their aptitude for being symbols and for being communicative from that antecedent tradition. Thus, such symbols—meant to represent thoughts, feelings, and so forth, in a form that can be perceived by our senses—

owe their capacity for representation to a linguistic tradition we carry within us that has already, to a great extent, determined their form and what they stand for.

I can check whether the words I use actually represent my thoughts. I notice that my thoughts, in the process of being represented by symbols of this kind, undergo changes: They may become clearer or more confused, or change direction. It seems—and this is perhaps a general characteristic of symbols—that whatever is represented by a symbol does not remain quite the same as before it was symbolized. Also, the symbol as provided by tradition undergoes subtle changes itself: it is used to represent a specific item in a specific context, and its representational import varies, if only slightly, with each occasion and with each writer (or speaker).

There are other expressions of inner processes and states that are not symbolic in the sense in which I have used the term in the proceding two paragraphs. A feeling of grief or anger may be expressed by sobbing or screaming. These and other expressions of emotions discharge inner tensions in an unmediated way, without the intermediary of symbols. Those mental processes we usually call thoughts, as distinguished from feelings, appear to require symbolic expression, indeed seem to depend on there being the possibility of such expression. In analysis we may ask the patient to put his discharge expressions into words, that is, to give them symbolic expression, or we may offer such an expression in the form of our words. Giving such symbolic expression is contingent on or conducive to having some distance from the inner state expressed. Unmediated expression may unintentionally communicate something about the experienced state to oneself or to someone else, but its primary function is release of tension. Secondarily, and then often pointedly, it may be used for communication to another person, as crying may become a means of demonstrating a wish to be soothed, or angry shouting a means for soliciting a counterattack. Early in life these discharge expressions are drawn into interactional context and communication, taking on the function of signals, as, for example, urinating (enuresis) and defecating often do.

Symbolism as so far discussed refers to the representation of some item by language. There is a symbolic relationship between *thing* and *word*, and the word seems to be nothing in its own right, nothing if not a symbol. However, the symbol concept as commonly used in psychoanalysis refers to a representational relationship between two items each of which is "real" in its own right; it is not the sole or primary function of one item to symbolize the other. In a frequently used example, snake as symbol for penis, we are dealing with two objects in nature which show an emotionally significant resemblance to each other, so that one may represent the other. Psychoanalysts distinguish between "archaic symbolism as a part of prelogical thinking, and distortion by means of representing a repressed idea through a conscious symbol. . . . Whereas in distortion the idea of penis is avoided through disguising it by the idea of snake, in prelogical thinking penis and snake are one and the same" (Fenichel 1945, p. 48). Although Jones acknowledged archaic symbolism as the genetic forerunner of what we call symbolism, for him true symbolism was characterized by the intervention of repression. Penis and snake, for prelogical thinking one and the same, in nonarchaic experience are separate entities; Jones and those who agree with him would claim that a symbolic relationship between the items is established when owing to their emotionally unacceptable resemblance the idea of penis is repressed. Thus a symbol would be an item that can represent in conscious thought another item the idea of which is repressed. In this view something properly is called a symbol in psychoanalysis if it stands in conscious thought for something else that is repressed, unconscious.

Clearly this is not the kind of symbolism we talked about before. The word-symbol presumably has no other function than to represent something else and has no meaning of its own. Also, words refer to, name, disclose what they represent; in their primary function they do not intend to conceal it, although they often enough do so secondarily. As every analyst knows, words help to evoke and bring to consciousness what they symbolize although they may disguise, blunt or sterilize it. It is worth noting however, that words and "things," like the snake and the penis, are sometimes equated in archaic mentation; the symbolic function of words, too, may ultimately derive from primitive sources of this kind. Jones and others use the term *symbolic equivalency* when refering to such archaic identity or exchangeability of symbol and symbolized. Werner and Kaplan call this *protosymbolism*. But when it comes to symbolism proper—where symbol and symbolized are differentiated from each other—there seems to be an unbridgeable gulf between the first symbol concept, exemplified by words, and the second, as used in psychoanalysis. If disguise is seen as the critical function of symbolic representation, if it is only that which is repressed that requires symbolization, what other disciplines mean by the term does not qualify as "true symbolism." Further reflection, however, seems to suggest that symbolization, as conceived by other disciplines, itself amounts to wishful disguise and distortion. Basic assumptions of traditional general psychoanalytic theory include the idea that representation as such disguises true psychic and material reality and its raw data. Thus it might be argued that psychoanalysis simply unmasks the true nature of symbolism, which other disciplines do not recognize. According to the broad concept of defense outlined earlier, under which sublimation is defined as a type of defense, the symbolism manifested in words and in other types of representation of a postulated objective reality would ultimately be defensive distortion.[1] If one accepts these basic theoretical assumptions concerning the nature of objective reality, then there is an inner logic to the argument. Since I do not accept them, I shall not pursue the matter further and will return to the discussion of psychoanalytic symbolism per se.

Objects, ideas, fantasies, events, or activities may acquire symbolic

1. This postulated objective reality here comprises so-called material reality and the "true psychic reality" of the unconscious. For Freud the raw data of unconscious life as revealed by psychoanalysis constituted objective psychic reality.

significance if they are connected in the mind with other such items in the manner that they stand in the relationship of representing them. A fantasy of having sexual intercourse with one's analyst may be symbolic of having intercourse with one's parent (and, conversely, the fantasy of having intercourse with a parent may symbolize intercourse with the analyst). The conscious fantasy stands for an unconscious one. The analyst is a symbol in Jones's sense when that fantasy has the function of defending against the unacceptable incestuous fantasy. In archaic mentation—for a schizophrenic, for example—having intercourse with the therapist and having intercourse with the parent are one and the same. In secondary-process mentation the two events and objects are distinguished. It must be emphasized that in the case of defense it is not a distinction or differentiation merely that has occurred between the two elements, but a *disjunction*; both elements may exist in consciousness side by side. The crucial factor in defense is the unconscious disruption of a connection between them—the disjunction of a significant link that had existed as the secondary-process heir of what had been in the archaic mentation, identity.

In my view, the representational relationship between symbol and symbolized—that is, their connection—can be consciously recognized without the result that the symbol ceases to be a symbol. On the contrary, the acknowledged connection now becomes a true symbolic relationship for the patient for the first time; the emotional significance of symbol and symbolized is activated in the patient. The symbol as instrument of defense—symbolism as disguise— stands revealed as a deficient variant of symbolization, one that is particularly relevant to psychoanalysis because of its importance for understanding neurosis and certain features of dreams. When, for instance, a patient gains the insight that the analyst in his or her fantasy or dream may function as a symbol for the father, the symbolic connection and the analyst's role as symbol do not cease to exist; indeed, both elements of the symbolism gain in meaning once there is conscious recognition of their symbolic relationship.

There is some justification for saying that we should speak of true symbolism, or symbolism proper, only when symbol and symbolized are clearly differentiated, which is not the case in archaic mentation. But it is unwarranted, I think, to maintain that *any* differentiation of symbol and symbolized is the work of repression and defense, or to hold that true symbolism, understood psychoanalytically, is not present unless repression is involved and the representational relationship of symbol and symbolized is disrupted. It does violence to language restricting the meaning of the word *symbolism* to the sphere of special psychoanalytic concerns. Alternatively, such a restriction may follow from the belief that all higher development of human mentation is a manifestation of defense against the unconscious, the instincts, and the exigencies of life. The same assumption is made when sublimation is understood as defense. Symbolization is a function, or activity, of universal range in human mentality. The word specifies an aspect of what *mind* means. The narrow definition of symbolism in psychoanalysis, as advocated by Jones and others at a comparatively early stage of psychoanalytic theory formation, bespeaks a far too narrow conception of psychoanalysis itself. Marion Milner (1952) has stated some of the disadvantages of cleaving to this narrow use of the concept in psychoanalysis:

> One of these is that it causes unnecessary confusion when one tries to communicate with workers in related disciplines, such as epistemology, aesthetics, and the philosophy of science; it interferes with what might be valuable collaboration in the work of clarifying some of the obscure issues about the nature of thought. This isolation of psychoanalysis, by its terminology, from related fields, may not have been a disadvantage in the early days of the struggle to establish analytic concepts in their own right, but now such isolation can, I think, lead to an impoverishment of our thinking. Another advantage of not limiting the meaning of the word symbol to a defensive function would be a clarification of theory by bringing it more in line with our practice. The analytic rule that the patient shall try to put all that he is aware of into words, does seem to imply a belief in the importance of

symbolization for maturity as well as for infancy; it implies the recognition that words are in fact symbols by means of which the world is comprehended. (p. 194)

Words as components of articulate verbal language are prominent among a variety of human productions that, in their mature form, intend to represent something other than what they "are" qua physical entities. On the other hand, neither the snake nor the analyst-qua-person intends to represent something or somebody else. (I am leaving aside here what may be called the analyst's technical intention to lend himself to the patient as a potential symbol of various object relations in the transference—an intention that addresses the patient's preexisting specific capacity for symbolization.)[2]

Clearly, there is a difference between the first and the second kind of symbols, but they are alike in being characterized by the representational relationship between symbol and symbolized. The symbolic link—the connection between symbol and symbolized—is disrupted or significantly weakened through the intervention of defenses. Language as a vehicle for symbolization also can be affected by defenses, so that the meaning of words—their symbolic valence—may be diminished or may even altogether disappear. Whatever course the defensive action takes, the symbol, whether an object (snake or analyst) or a word, stands more or less by itself, becomes defective as symbol. But—to put it pointedly—it would follow according to the strict definition advocated by Jones, that it then *becomes* a symbol.

How can we understand this contradiction? The Jonesian concept implies that a symbol intimates something hidden, that what is symbolized hovers in the unconscious background and in some way determines the appearance of the symbol. For the person who uses (what the analyst recognizes as) a symbol the symbolic link is neither

---

2. One may say that in this regard the analyst intentionally functions as a cipher, a nonentity to be invested with meaning by the patient.

conscious nor "conscient"[3] but is operative instead in a hidden way. Without this hidden connectedness the symbolizing item would not appear in consciousness at the time when it does; it could not be used, as it were, for defensive purposes. This is best formulated by saying that it is the symbolic *linkage* which is repressed. Repression, far from bringing symbolism about, disguises symbolism by interfering with the symbolic linkage and hiding the symbolic function of the symbol. Defense is responsible not for creating symbolism, but for disrupting it, disguising it, and distorting it.

I have said that the symbol—an object, idea, fantasy, or image, for example—does not cease to be symbolic when repression is lifted. When that occurs the patient in analysis recognizes a meaningful correspondence between the symbol and the symbolized. The symbol becomes a symbol *for him*, whereas before the lifting of repression it had not been. The analyst can surmise the symbol-function of the item in question because he does not repress the linkage to what is symbolized. In the case of the patient who dreams of intercourse with the analyst, in becoming conscious of the dream's symbolic meaning he establishes a manifest connection between two fantasies. The unconscious fantasy (intercourse with father) is not lifted from repression simply by appearing as an item of conscious thought alongside another item of thought (intercourse with analyst). The intent and—under favorable circumstances—the effect of the interpretation "Your dream of intercourse with me stands for the fantasy of intercourse with your father" is to revive the unconscious identity or equivalence of the two fantasies in the archaic depth of the psyche, through a consciously experienced connection that is a reflection, an articulate repossession, of that identity.

In his paper "The Unconscious," Freud writes: "If we communicate to a patient some idea which he has at one time repressed but which we have discovered in him, our telling him makes at first no

3. For my use of this term, see Loewald [1976], 1980, p. 169; it is a substitute for *preconscious*.

change in his mental condition. Above all, it does not remove the repression nor undo its effects, as might perhaps be expected from the fact that the previously unconscious idea has now become conscious." And a few lines later: "Actually there is no lifting of the repression until the conscious idea, after the resistances have been overcome, has *entered into connection* with the unconscious memory-trace" [my italics]. And further: "The identity of the information given to the patient with his repressed memory is only apparent. To have heard something and to have experienced something are in their psychological nature two quite different things, even though the content of both is the same" (1915b, pp. 175–76). Later in the same paper he writes: "Now . . . we are in a position to state precisely what it is that repression denies to the rejected presentation in the transference neuroses:. . . . translation into words which shall remain attached to the object" (ibid., p. 202). It is quite significant in our present context that an accurate translation of the last clause of the German text actually would be: "translation into words which shall remain *connected* with the object" [my italics].[4] The symbol, whether a word or a symbolizing fantasy or dream symbol, disguises what it symbolizes if the *connection* between symbol and symbolized is repressed. This is a deficient mode of symbolism. Symbolism is fully restored if the connection gets reestablished.

We encounter a different "deficient mode" of symbolism at the other end of the spectrum in the symbolic equivalency evidenced in "archaic symbolism as a part of prelogical thinking" (Fenichel). This is akin to Werner and Kaplan's protosymbolism, to which I referred earlier. Protosymbolism, or archaic symbolism, plays an important part in primitive mentation of various kinds. The deficiency here consists in failure to differentiate symbolized and symbol. The representational linkage is not severed, as in repression, so as to produce two disconnected elements. Instead, in archaic mentation the *pre-*

4. The original text: *"Die Uebersetzung in Worte, welche mit dem Objekt verknuepft bleiben sollen"* (1940–68, G.W. 10:300).

conditions for linkage do not obtain: the two elements, distinguished in advanced mentation, here remain, or become again, one—or blend, so as to be indistinguishable. One does not *represent* the other, it *is* the other "in substantial actuality" (Ferenczi 1911, p. 137). We see indications of this mode of thinking in the concreteness of schizophrenic thought and speech and in psychotic transferences and, in less pronounced form, in the concerns of children and neurotic adults about the magic of thoughts and words. For the schizophrenic there is neither a felt link between differentiated items of experience nor a disruption of that link; rather, archaic oneness of experiences is retained, or can easily be reestablished, and can be conscious.

A schizophrenic patient in psychotherapy with me had spoken during a session about her long-standing sexual relations with her father. With a meaningful glance at me, she then fell silent. When I asked her what she was thinking, she merely said quietly, "Come over" (we were facing each other), beckoning me to do so. For her at that moment, there was no difference between her father and me. In that moment, before I had a chance to say anything to her, the door to my office opened and, in full view of the patient, a drug salesman stuck his head in, muttering something about samples he wanted to leave with me. I got up from my chair, told him to go away, and returned to my chair. Then the patient and I laughed in relief: The psychotic spell was broken. For the patient, just before the interruption by the *deus ex machina*, it had not been a question of a (symbolic) connection between two situations or fantasies—of a connection between memory and actuality, between past and present. For her the two had been one and the same, or perhaps one merged into the other in seamless continuity. What for me were two significantly related but separate situations, for her were not differentiated, and thus she could not connect them to each other in thought. Although later in the hour she could grasp the symbolic connection, at that moment in which I had become for her the live partner of her intimate life—a moment carrying the intensity of actuality—the symbolic relationship between two experiences had collapsed into a unitary experience. Her capacity for symbolization had become inoperative—not by a defensive disruption of the connection between the two experiences, but by their archaic merging into one.[5]

It is the capacity for symbolization that clinical psychoanalysis promotes, usually by progressively leading the patient from repressed symbolism to actualizing and verifying live symbolic connections between hitherto disparate items of experience and thought. "Mutative" transference interpretations (Strachey 1934) are particularly apt to be convincing in this regard. When a neurotic patient gains emotional insight through a transference interpretation, two experiences become linked in a psychic act that is achieved by means of a symbolizing bridge provided by the analyst's words. What distinguishes words (and sentences, in which the words themselves are mutually connected) from a symbolic object such as a snake or the analyst is that language is not simply a system of symbols for "things" but a symbolizing instrumentality by which the symbolic potentiality of "things" (that is, of entities of one kind or another) is brought to the fore. Words are not symbols merely in the sense that they are objective units that can be heard or read and that represent things; more important, they are themselves symbolizing links that establish or reestablish connections between items of experience. Words are vocal and written embodiments of the symbolizing activity itself—that is, not just of items of experience but of the experiencing activity. Language has such a special status in symbolism because it is a prime function and intention of words to provide, to *be*, bridges between

---

5. My account of this particular episode, as well as of the deficient mode of symbolization in archaic mentation in general, is not contradicted by the view that factors of patients' resistance are at work here too. Broadly speaking, they would fall into the rubric of what Freud has called the resistance of the id and has explained by the compulsion to repeat (1926, pp. 159–60). One can, at least in a number of cases, understand a patient's sliding back into an archaic mode of mentation as a clinging to that undifferentiated level. For duscussions on id resistance and repetition compulsion see my *Papers on Psychoanalysis* (1980, especially pp. 38–39, 65–68, and 87–101).

items of experience other than themselves and to bring out connections between them. If the crucial factor in repression is the unconscious disruption of connections between elements of experience, words have the potential for undoing this disjunction. As symbolizing bridges they articulate differences and, in that function, may be characterized as joints (the word *articulate* derives from the Latin *artus*, "joint"): they indicate differences and separateness while in the same act pointing at junction, relatedness.[6]

To the extent to which in archaic mentation there is deficiency of differentiation, words tend to lose their symbolizing function; they are equated with what they are intended to symbolize and become protosymbols. As interpersonal communication too, language accentuates relatedness in difference. Where there is unconscious or intense wordless communication, words become irrelevant. For a schizophrenic, for instance, his or her own words and those of the therapist may become protosymbols. Alternatively, for the patient the therapist's words may have no meaning, may not link anything, and may not even maintain a viable connection between the patient and the therapist in his role as a symbolizing agent. Here words cease to function as symbols of communication itself.

In summary, word-symbols in their more advanced form of functioning differentiate and connect (and so integrate) items of experience. In interpersonal communication, words make manifest difference and relatedness between the participants, they are symbol bridges between addressor and addressee—symbolizing not only what the words refer to but also the closeness-in-distance of the communicants.

For the deeply regressed schizophrenic, language may not suffice as the main medium of differentiating-connecting symbolization; more substantial, less fragile bridges may be needed at times. M.-A. Séchehaye's "symbolic realization" (1951a, 1951b) is pertinent here. Mme. Séchehaye writes of apples, which she gave to a female schizo-

---

6. For a relevant brief discussion of words, see Freud's short paper "The Antithetical Meaning of Primal Words" (1910c, pp. 155–61).

phrenic patient in psychotherapy with her as symbols of the mother therapist breast, which functioned as archaic protosymbols. Such protosymbols, in this respect like Winnicott's transitional objects, must not be challenged with the question of either-or; whether these apples *are* what for us they symbolize or whether they *represent* the symbolized—posing this alternative cannot do justice to the phenomenon. Apples would be particularly apt to fulfill such an ambiguous function, so could be concrete embodiments of a vital gift from the mother/therapist; succulent and shaped like breasts, they give oral nourishment. They are apple-breasts in a substantial way that cannot be matched by the word *breast*. Equally inappropriate is the question whether the therapist functions as a symbol for—represents—the mother or whether he or she *is* the mother at such times. We must add that on archaic levels of mentation differentiation between mother and baby, between breast and sucking mouth, is also deficient. Because they have that twilight valence, these apples can help the patient, under favorable circumstances, to initiate differentiation and connection between breast and apple, between mother and therapist, as well as between patient and therapist.[7] Words spoken to the patient by the therapist in predominantly verbal psychotherapy—and a fortiori in psychoanalysis—are no longer, as was the case in infancy, embedded in or fused with concrete bodily interactions between mother and infant (see my paper on language, Loewald [1978] 1980, pp. 178–206). Separated from this matrix, words and the verbal inter-

---

7. A kindred symbolic realization is the Eucharist. The various theological explications, by different Christian churches, of the Sacrament (as *transsubstantiation, consubstantiation,* or simply *symbolic*) show the difficulties involved if such a rite and its materials are questioned as to whether they *are* the real thing or only *represent* it. Also, it may not be too farfetched to suggest that transferences in analysis and the transference neurosis show a comparable kind of ambiguity. Transferences are interpreted by the analyst as symbolic repetitions of old attachments and conflicts, while the patient has a tendency to regard the same phenomena as experiences in present actuality. When Freud said in "The Dynamics of Transference" (1912a) that "it is impossible to destroy anyone *in absentia* or *in effigie*" (p. 108), he alluded to the necessity for symbolic realization.

pretations of the therapist may be articulating joints of which the regressed schizophrenic patient cannot make use and which therefore become for him or her empty shells, devoid of meaning and having no valence at all.

There are two extremes: words become mere sounds without meaning, or they do not represent their referents but are merged with them. As in all matters of developmental levels, boundaries—here between symbolic equivalency, protosymbolism, and symbolism proper—are ambiguous and fluid, and so are boundaries between the symbolic character and the meaninglessness of words. Fluidity and ambiguity of boundaries between symbolism proper and the two modes of deficient symbolism characterizes, of course, not only word-symbols, but also symbolism in general. It should be understood that the two deficient modes of symbolization are termed deficient as measured against a norm of sanity where oscillations between the two poles of "psychotic" (protosymbolism) and "neurotic" (defense) deviations are moderate and readily reversible. The word *deficient* here is not meant to imply that these two modes do not have their own valid standing and importance in the total spectrum of mentation; they are, I repeat, living elements of a sanity which has not become a caricature of itself.

Psychoanalysis, as a specific method of psychotherapy, proceeds in the medium of language, and the common ground for analyst and analysand is their agreement about the symbolic, rather than protosymbolic, and the revealing, rather than concealing, function of the words they use. But boundaries here, too, are not firm, and the balance and agreement are easily disturbed. The implicit agreement about the nature of symbolism frequently cannot be honored by the patient in the heat of passion and defense and may need to be restored with the help of the analyst. The same is true, as we know from the vicissitudes of transference and resistance, regarding agreements about other, nonverbal, interactions in analysis and regarding the symbolic significance of the patient's fantasies, memories, and thoughts.

Werner and Kaplan, in their book on symbol formation (1963), briefly discuss the term *symbol*:

> In regard to the term 'symbol' we note. . . . the wide range of meaning this word has in common usage. The distinctive mark of the concept as employed here is its inherent duality: . . . a symbol entails a "vehicle" which, through its particular form and qualitative properties, represents a "referent", that is, an object, a concept, or a thought. "Representation" in the sense used here implies more than simple and direct expression of meaning by a vehicle: it implies some awareness, however vague, that vehicle and referential object are not identical but are, in substance and form, two totally different entities. Thus a name, when handled—as in magic—entirely as the thing it ordinarily represents, is no more a "symbol" than the object itself. Similarly, a gesture directly and unintentionally expressing an emotion such as joy or disgust is not symbolic; the so-called "symbolism" of gestural and postural patterns may be symbolic for the interpreter, but they are not for the producing individual. Again, the "latent thought" of dream images may render these images symbolic for the interpreting psychotherapist; for the dreamers, the dream images are taken as such and are thus not symbolic. From true symbols we distinguish. . . . those productions whereby the vehicular structures (imagery, visual or verbal patterns, gestures, etc.) "present" a meaning rather than "represent" it. One might call these productions *protosymbols*. Though on the surface often indistinguishable from true symbols, protosymbols lack the *intentional* act by which a vehicular form is taken to represent a referent. Nevertheless, protosymbols are extremely important in the genetic processes of symbolization: protosymbols may be transformed into true symbols by progressive differentiation of vehicle and referential meaning; true symbolism may regress to protosymbols through de-differentiation of vehicle and referent. (Pp. 16–17; italics in the original)

Depending on the predilections of the theorist, either protosymbolism or the defensive disjunction of symbol and symbolized may be regarded as "true symbolism." In my view both should be seen as deficient modes of symbolism which, however, greatly contribute to the understanding of symbolization.

Freud, in his short paper "An Evidential Dream" (1913a) pointed out that obsessional neurosis is "a condition which, from what I have observed, makes it considerably harder to understand dream-symbols, just as dementia praecox makes it easier" (p. 275). This is true in the first case, I believe, in great part due to the defensive disjunction of symbol and symbolized, in the second case to the fusion of symbol and symbolized. In the section called "Representation by Symbols in Dreams", a 1914 addition to "The Interpretation of Dreams," Freud comments on the "to a large extent still unsolved problems attaching to the concept of a symbol." He goes on to say that cases where "the element in common between a symbol and what it represents [is concealed], must be able to throw light upon the ultimate meaning of the symbolic relation, and they indicate that it is of a genetic character. Things that are symbolically connected today were probably united in prehistoric times [(Urzeiten)] by conceptual and linguistic identity. The symbolic relation seems to be a relic and a mark of former identity." He adds, "Dreams make use of this symbolism for the disguised representation of their latent thoughts" (pp. 351–52).

Helen Keller in *The Story of My Life* (1903) gives a vivid and moving description of symbolization in action and its impact on her emotional-intellectual life. Her account was called to my attention by Werner and Kaplan (1963); it is also referred to in E. Rodrigué's "Notes on Symbolism" (1956). At the time of this incident, as is well known, Helen Keller, deaf and blind from the age of two years, was being educated to use language by her teacher, Anne Sullivan.

> One day, while I was playing with my new doll, Miss Sullivan put my big rag doll [an old familiar one] into my lap also, spelled "d-o-l-l" and tried to make me understand that "d-o-l-l" applied to both. Earlier in

the day we had had a tussle over the words "m-u-g" and "w-a-t-e-r". Miss Sullivan had tried to impress upon me that "m-u-g" is *mug* and that "w-a-t-e-r" is *water*, but I persisted in confounding the two. In despair she had dropped the subject for the time, only to renew it at the first opportunity. I became impatient of her repeated attempts and, seizing the new doll, I dashed it upon the floor. I was keenly delighted when I felt the fragments of the broken doll at my feet. Neither sorrow nor regret followed my passionate outburst. I had not loved the doll. In the still, dark world in which I lived there was no strong sentiment or tenderness. . . .

[Later that same day] We walked down the path to the well-house, attracted by the fragrance of the honeysuckle with which it was covered. Someone was drawing water and my teacher placed my hand under the spout. As the cool stream gushed over one hand she spelled into the other the word water, first slowly, then rapidly. I stood still, my whole attention fixed upon the motions of her fingers. Suddenly I felt a misty consciousness as of something forgotten—a thrill of returning thought; and somehow the mystery of language was revealed to me. I knew then that "w-a-t-e-r" meant the wonderful cool something that was flowing over my hand. The living word awakened my soul, gave it light, hope, joy, set it free! There were barriers still, it is true, but barriers that in time could be swept away. . . . I left the well-house eager to learn. Everything had a name, and each name gave birth to a new thought. As we returned to the house, every object which I touched seemed to quiver with life. That was because I saw everything with the strange new sight that had come to me. (Pp. 36–37)

These two episodes in their juxtaposition are remarkable in many respects; I shall focus here on the issue of symbolism. In the view of Werner and Kaplan, "The unique value of Helen Keller's retrospective statements lies in the unmistakable proof that names are symbols that connote, represent, or depict, and as such are *toto caelo* set apart from signs which label things or direct behavior. . . . Miss Keller's account attests to the superficiality of the notion that it is a contiguous connection which binds the symbol and the referent; her beautiful description documents the very *shift of function* from signal to symbol." They continue:

> One might probe further and ask the question: what may have been the critical elements in the events at the well which brought about the sudden understanding of the symbolic function? We doubt that a conclusive answer can ever be given. We may, however, . . . at least offer some conjecture as to the potent factors inherent in that memorable event. . . . In the "mug" situation, there was an entirely external connection between a static object and certain tactual signs. In the "water" situation, the object was itself an *event:* the flowing of cool water over the hand. And as Miss Sullivan "poured" the tactual signs over one of Helen's hands, and the cool liquid over the other, there perhaps occurred two tactual experiences that may have been internally linked in the child's mind—a linkage based on common dynamic features: "water" comes to mean the "cool something flowing over the hand." (Pp. 110–12; italics in original)

In addition, I suggest that it may have been significant as an ingredient of the total experience that the event at the well took place in an atmosphere of good smells and serenity—in contrast to the earlier mug and doll episodes in which Helen and Anne had been impatient and irritated. It also should be noted that *water* had been one of the few words known to Helen before her disabling illness (see Keller 1903, p. 19). Perhaps—as she seems to intimate in the above account—a link with an early memory was established in the current experience. The authors' ingenious description of Miss Sullivan's "pouring" the tactual signs over one hand while water poured over the other points to a unison of the two emotionally poignant sensations, experienced by one human organism simultaneously—in different yet symmetrical and closely correlated organs. One may assume that the complex confluence of symmetrical sensations, early memory (of water), and harmony with her teacher and the environment enabled Helen to grasp, or recreate, a symbolic connection that showed unity-in-difference and difference-in-unity.

Helen Keller claims that "that living word awakened my soul, gave it light, hope, joy, set it free." She now could generalize: "Everything had a name, and each name gave birth to a new thought. . . . every object which I touched seemed to quiver with life. That was because I saw everything with the strange new sight that had come to me." I find it impossible to avoid thinking here of Freud's *hypercathexis* which consists in a linking of "thing-presentation" with "the word-presentations corresponding to it." These hypercathexes "bring about a higher psychical organization and make it possible for the primary process to be suceeded by the secondary process" (1915b, p. 202)—the "strange new sight" that had come to Helen.[8]

8. In my paper "Primary Process, Secondary Process, and Language" ([1978] 1980, pp. 178–206) I have proposed that the underlying correspondence of word presentations to the thing presentation—which makes pertinent linking of the two elements possible—is rooted in archaic experiences of identity of "thing" and "word" (the articulating word sounds coming from the mother). In that paper some phenomena and problems of symbolism are further discussed, as is the concept of hypercathexis.

CHAPTER FIVE

Illusion

Let me briefly return at this point to my characterization of symbolization as "an imaginative act: two different items of experience are linked in the mind in such a way that one represents the other." I stressed what I called then the "subjective" nature of the representational relationship, which consists in the fact that the symbol is always a symbol *for us*, whereas objects, events, and processes and nonsymbolic relations between objects or events, and the like, are perceived as existing in some kind of objective universe. We have to remember, however, that we include in this objective universe temporal-spatial relations between items, for example, although they clearly have much to do with the schemata our mind brings to the material of experience. In the case of symbolism we are more or less aware of the part played by our subjective mental processes, while in the case of perception in general and of temporal-spatial relations we are for the most part not cognizant of the mind's "schematism" (so termed by Kant). This noncognizance—paradoxical as it may seem—is due to the dominance of secondary-process mentation in our ordinary perceptual and thought processes. We tend to take for granted this more highly developed form of mentation and to assume its results to be features of the "objective" world, although actually it contributes to the organization of the world as objective. Symbolism, more closely in touch with primary process, is seen as subjective in contrast to the objective world of secondary process.

Illusion. The imaginative activity of symbolization appears to be subjective in a special way—the symbolism deriving either from an individual subject or from the collective subjectivity of a cultural group or of the human race in toto. Human imagination may lose itself in flights of fancy and easily depart from the solid ground of observation and facts. As "pure imagination" it is akin to illusion and delusion: something exists "only in our imagination." If symbolization is called an imaginative activity, this may suggest that in symbolism we deal with mere figments of the imagination. On the other hand, an *image* is the more or less faithful portrayal or reproduction, or the presentation or representation, of an object in external reality. A mental image (one of the senses of the German *Vorstellung,* also translated as "representation") of an object in external reality is an inner, subjective semblance of the external object. Thus, human imagination, construed as the faculty that builds and maintains inner images of external objects, is understood as our trusted guide in dealing with the external object-world (see Rapaport's concept of the "inner map," 1967, n. 17, p. 696. Imagination is a two-edged instrument: it may closely adhere and conform to objective reality or wildly deviate from and distort it.

Every psychoanalyst knows the Scylla and Charybdis between which we perilously steer our course in making interpretations or reconstructions: our imagination may mislead us into unfounded assumptions about a patient's experience and motivations, but if we are lacking imagination we will not get at his experience and will leave it untouched. Without imagination we will fail to bring out the symbolic significance of his experience and verbal reports and will remain remote from the patient's psychic reality and its symbolizing universe. The analyst's imagination is here an indispensable instrument with which we perceive and test that universe. That is to say, it is our own symbolizing activity which makes it possible to apprehend the patient's symbolic universe in its outlines and to "test" it. (It may be noted that this is also a statement about "empathy").

Through our imaginative work of symbolizing, the patient's symbolic universe—the whole open-ended network of his representational links, which constitutes an important dimension of his psychic reality—becomes accessible to us as an object of study and of therapeutic influence. If psychic reality is a legitimate area of systematic scientific study and if the investigator's concordant activity of symbolizing is the instrument through which man's symbolizing activity and its productions become available, then there is nothing unscientific or nonobjective involved here. In the same way man studies the physical universe: it becomes available to him via the instrument of his own physical-biological activities and its extensions, which are concordant with the forces and motions of the physical-biological world.

If the patient's symbolic universe accounts for an important part of the data of his psychic reality one wishes to investigate—the status of such data is comparable to that of the data of material reality. Illusion enters the arena if the investigator's imagination, for whatever reasons, leads him to misapprehend or "imagine" data. Imagination— the faculty that forms mental images or reproductions of the actual data of psychic or material reality—more or less faithfully reproduces these realities. Illusion is possible insofar as our mental images may be not faithful but distorted reproductions or may even be "caused" by purely subjective processes in the perceiver, without having any basis in a reality outside that person.

The problem of illusion shifts, however, when we ask whether or to what extent psychic reality (including its symbolic universe) corresponds or conforms to material physical reality. For example, under various circumstances our subjective sense of time, a phenomenon of psychic reality, is different from clock time. Measured by the standard of clock time, we often suffer from illusions about the passage of time. A time span, in our "subjective" experience, may be longer or shorter than it is in "objective" time. This deception may arise due to one's emotional state during that period of time: when one is bored, for instance, the time seems longer than the objectively measured time; if one is absorbed in an activity the time seems shorter. In both instances we are likely to say that one is under an illusion. A hallucinated face or voice, although it may be that of a real person, is a vivid materialization of someone not actually present in material reality. Waking up from a vivid dream, and so reestablishing contact with and orientation in the external world, makes us realize that we were under a delusion; reality testing is restored with a return to the world of shared presences and shared standards, or indices, of reality. (For the purposes of this discussion I make no sharp distinction between illusion and delusion.) The illusion that time has passed more quickly than, according to clock time, it has may be called a subjective or emotionally motivated illusion, one perhaps shared by other persons absorbed in the same activity. But we speak of illusion also in a different sense—that applicable to optical illusions, for example. A mirage may be seen by all those present in a certain place at a certain time, irrespective of the inner state or emotional condition of the observers. In some cases a mirage like a hullucination, may have the vividness and may carry the conviction of objective reality. Only our trusted memory of the actual lay of the land leads us, in a reflective act, to the convincing conclusion that despite all appearances this is an illusion: we trust our memory here more than we trust the evidence of our sense peception. We may know that the phenomenon often is brought about by certain atmospheric conditions. The urgent conviction of its reality may be enhanced by subjective wishes and needs, as in the case of the exhausted wanderer in the desert being confronted by the mirage of an oasis; the need for water may even move him to hallucinate an oasis without the presence of mospheric conditions that can conspire with the wish. One the other hand, the factor of wish fulfillment may be weak or entirely absent in such illusions.

Freud, in the context of "The Future of an Illusion," made the wish-fulfillment motive the decisive criterion for the concept. He went so far as to claim that illusion—here the example is religious belief—is not primarily characterized by being an error as compared with the true facts—although the belief in question *is* usually erroneous—but by the overwhelming subjective motive of wish fulfillment. Illusion became for him a belief about the external world which is subjectively determined, regardless of its conformity to objective facts (Freud 1927, pp. 30–31). I claim, on the contrary, that *being deceived about the reality of something* is central to illusion, whether the deception is due to inner or to external factors or to both. Illusion is a form of error when measured against a standard of truth we take as absolute. If it emerges that a belief we had thought was an illusion actually conforms to that standard, then it reveals itself not to have been an illusion after all. For Freud, however, it remains an illusion as long as it was engendered or embraced because of wishes opposed to and defenses against what seemed to be the true state of affairs at the time of its occurrence.

Thus, psychoanalysis tends to adhere to narrow, idiosyncratic explanations and definitions of both symbolism and illusion: the concepts are tied to defense and wish fulfillment.

Winnicott deals with symbolism and illusion in an original but not altogether satisfactory way. In "Transitional Objects and Transitional Phenomena" (1953) he stakes out a claim for a "third part of the life of a human being," in addition to external and inner reality. This third part "is an intermediate area of *experiencing*, to which inner reality and external life both contribute. It is an area which is not challenged, because no claim is made on its behalf except that it shall exist as a resting-place for the individual engaged in the perpetual human task of keeping inner and outer reality separate yet inter-related" (Winnicott's italics). The transitional object is an example, an embodiment as it were, of that intermediate area—of "an intermediate state between a baby's inability and growing ability to recognize and accept reality" (inner *and* outer reality as separate though interrelated). He continues:

> I am therefore studying the substance of *illusion*, that which is al-
> lowed to the infant, and which in adult life is inherent in art and
> religion, and yet becomes the hallmark of madness when an adult
> puts too powerful a claim on the credulity of others, forcing them to

acknowledge a sharing of illusion that is not their own. We can share a respect for *illusory experience,* and if we wish we may collect together and form a group on the basis of the similarity of our illusory experiences. This is a natural root of grouping among human beings. (P. 90; Winnicott's italics)

This "third part of the life of a human being," the "intermediate area between the subjective and that which is objectively perceived" (ibid.), according to Winnicott pertains to "the substance of illusion". But, we may ask, is experiencing (in Winnicott's sense) the substance of illusion, or is experiencing rather the root and the playground of both reality and illusion? Indeed, one may say that this "intermediate area" makes possible the distinction, as well as the confusion, between inner and outer reality. Winnicott appears to claim that experiencing is an area between inner and outer reality, which both contribute to it, and, further, that this third area is the province of illusion. But it is the separation into outer and inner reality that makes for the possibility of "reality" and "illusion." Prior to sorting out inner and outer reality there is no "room" for an intermediate third area, no space in which to distinguish or oppose illusion and reality. Winnicott describes the area of cultural experience as an extension or expansion of the transitional phenomena of childhood—an acceptable formulation, in my view. In adult organization of mental life, as it is generally conceived, we can think in terms of "areas." But insofar as in the area of cultural experience the dichotomy of inner and outer reality is suspended or nonoperative, here too there is no "space" for distinguishing illusion and reality.

Experiencing, as exemplified in transitional phenomena, cannot be said to be either illusory or nonillusory. Because they exist prior to or beyond that dichotomy, transitional phenomena cannot be challenged with such an alternative. Winnicott is interested in the relationship of the transitional objects to symbolism.

When symbolism is employed the infant is already clearly distinguishing between fantasy and fact, between inner objects and external objects, between primary creativity and perception. But the term transitional object, according to my suggestion, gives room for the process of becoming able to accept difference and similarity. I think there is use for a term for the root of symbolism in time, a term that describes the infant's journey from the purely subjective to objectivity; and it seems to me that the transitional object . . . is what we see of this journey . . . (1953, p. 92)

He then refers to the variable meaning of the term *symbolism* and to the growth of the individual as traced in his movement from what has been called symbolic equivalence or protosymbolism to symbolism proper. In this context he discusses the wafer of the Blessed Sacrament as symbol of the body of Christ; for Roman Catholics the wafer *is* the body, whereas for Protestants it is—as Winnicott puts it—a substitute, a reminder, and not actually the body itself. Genuine Roman Catholic experience adheres to symbolic equivalence, Protestant experience is built on more fully developed symbolism. Winnicott thinks of the transitional object as a tangible marker of this journey from symbolic equivalence to symbolism proper, and "from the purely subjective to objectivity."

Some of his terms and conceptual formulations, I believe, despite the admirable originality and aptness of his observations do not do full justice to his findings. For instance, when he writes of the transitional object that it is what we see of "the infant's journey from the purely subjective to objectivity", he uses terms that in my view are not applicable at this level of experience. The journey does not start from the subjective; it is a journey from a state prior to the differentiation of subjectivity and objectivity to a state when subjectivity and objectivity come into being. Transitional objects and phenomena are transitional not by virtue of being in transit from the subjective to objectivity, but insofar as they represent way stations from indeterminacy to determinacy or from the ineffable to the effable.

Of the transitional object it can be said that it is a matter of agreement between us and the baby that we will never ask the question "Did you conceive of this or was it presented to you from without?" The important point is that no decision on this point is expected. The question is not to be formulated. (This whole passage is in italics in the original. Winnicott 1953, p. 95.)

If this question is not to be formulated even at the way station of the transitional object, so much less must a decision on the question "subjective or objective?" be implied for the time when the baby "perceives" the maternal breast. But this implication is made when the journey Winnicott posits is characterized as one beginning with the purely subjective. Such a formulation has "decided" that the infant's "primary creativity"—the step in which the infant is ready to create the maternal breast just where and when the mother offers the actual breast (Winnicott 1953, p. 95)—is a phenomenon of subjectivity. One faces a dilemma in that it is the hallmark of such states that they are neutral in respect to subjectivity and objectivity, but scientific language seems to demand or presuppose a decision one way or the other. Therefore scientific language, as commonly understood, is inadequate here: descriptions and conceptualizations have to be couched in often self-contradictory circumlocutions and formulated with the help of analogies, metaphors, and negative terms.[1] Unsatisfactory as these alternatives may be, it is unnecessarily misleading to speak of the infant's primary creativity as purely subjective.

On the subject of illusion, Winnicott writes: "The mother's adaptation to the infant's needs, when good enough, gives the infant the *illusion* that there is an external reality that corresponds to the infant's own capacity to create" (ibid., p. 95; Winnicott's italics). He also says, "The mother, at the beginning, by almost 100 per cent. adaptation affords the infant the opportunity for the *illusion* that her breast is part of the infant. . . . The mother's eventual task is gradually to disillusion the infant, but she has no hope for success unless at first she has been able to give sufficient opportunity for illusion" (ibid. pp. 94–95. Winnicott's italics). The various descriptions he gives of this early

---

1. The word *neutral* itself uses negation; so does the word *unconscious*.

stage and its dynamics in this paper, and the role played by illusion, can be summed up as follows: The infant is allowed the illusion that the mother's breast ("external reality") is created by the infant, and the mother is allowed the illusion that the infant is a creation of hers. These are illusions of subjective creation obtaining in both of them. In the weaning process a necessary gradual disillusionment is occurring in the infant as well as in the mother (although Winnicott does not comment on the latter). "Primary creativity" (omnipotence) in both is gradually cut down to size—the size of a later truth—with attending frustration and grief, as well as a developing sense—both joyous and sad—of subjectivity and objectivity. It is on acquisition of this later truth that we judge the earlier one to be an illusion. Illusion, according to the *Oxford English Dictionary*, is a deception, mocking us. Are baby and mother illuding themselves and each other about the true state of affairs—perhaps a shared illusion? Or is it the truth at that deep level of mentation which is called here illusion? What from the perspectives of secondary process and the distinction of subjectivity and objectivity is seen as an illusion is the truth of creativity, which does not raise the specter of "inner" and "outer"; and the truth of subjectivity-objectivity from the perspective of primary process and oneness is seen as an illusion. Perhaps a binocular vision that takes both viewpoints seriously, without partiality, may bring us closer to elusive truth than either vision in isolation. The fact that we speak of illusion in regard to the processes discussed is mainly a sign of the inadequacy both of the human mind and of language, which impels us to measure one vision by the other.

Winnicott's description of the infants creating the breast just where and when the maternal breast appears is applicable, mutatis mutandis, to artist and artistic medium. The poet creates new language just where word sounds and word shapes present themselves to him. Elsewhere I have attempted to describe this encounter as follows: "It is the momentum of an active imaginative process that creates the next step [in artistic production], propelled by the directional tension of the previous steps. This directional tension is the resultant of the artist's imagination and the inherent force of his medium. A word, a sound, a color, a shape—in the case of dramatic art an action—, or a sequence of these, once determined, strongly suggests the next step to be taken" (Loewald 1980, "Psychoanalysis as an Art," p. 369). Of the good analytic hour I said that there "patient and analyst . . . become both artist and medium for each other. For the analyst as artist his medium is the patient . . . ; for the patient as artist the analyst becomes his medium., . . . as living human media they have their own creative capabilities, so that they are both creators themselves" (ibid.) and upon each other. One may say that the maternal breast is the medium of the infant's creative tension even as the infant in its creative tension is the medium of the mother's creative breast. I do not wish to leave the impression that I consider the dynamic reciprocal engagement under discussion as unique to creative art and deeply meaningful personal encounters. It also takes place, although most often in derivative and corrupted ways, in ordinary living; and it plays a central part in original scientific work no less than in artistic creation.[2]

2. The work of art—a poem, symphony, painting, sculpture, play, or novel—once completed, gains an existence of its own not unlike the transitional object of infancy; it becomes an embodiment of the engaging tensions that have engendered it. As an "art object" it has become a significant element and expression of the common world of artist and audience and begins to have a life that is no longer strictly tied to the artist's omnipotence. It acquires characteristics of an object of nature, as well as a history of its own. There are artists for whom parting with their product is very difficult, much as a child is reluctant to give up a blanket or teddy bear or to share toys with other children. The journey undertaken in differentiating between subjectivity and objectivity is not an easy one—it requires differentiation not only between self and others as persons but also between self and a world of things no longer under omnipotent-magical control. When the creator's consent to this objectivation is achieved to a significant degree, he is able to turn his attention to new imaginative work—having allowed such detachment to take its course. Winnicott's discussion of *illusion-disillusionment* (1953, pp. 95–96) is pertinent here, as is what he writes about the "fate" of the transitional object (ibid., p. 91). But in view of my discussion of the concept of *illusion*, I should prefer to speak, rather than of *illusion* and *disillusionment*, of *enchantment* and *disenchantment*. (I shall return to this formulation later in the text.)

CHAPTER SIX

Subjectivity

*L*et me repeat: I do not think that the infant is allowed the illusion of having created the breast ("external reality"), that is, the illusion that the external world is his own subjective creation, by virtue of the mother's presenting the breast just where and when the infant needs it. There are as yet no subjective and external worlds to have illusions about. Perhaps we can come closer to an adequate understanding by introducing the concept of *invention* here. Mother and infant may be said to invent each other in the mouth-breast encounter: they come upon something and, out of need or desire, invent—jointly—its utilization. According to *Webster's New International Dictionary* (2d ed.), "One invents by forming combinations which are either entirely new, or which attain their ends by means unknown before. One discovers what had existed before, but had remained unknown." The infant is not allowed the illusion of having created the breast, nor does he discover the breast as something preexisting but hitherto unknown to him; rather, infant/mother invents the mouth-breast "combination," which comes into existence in the manner of a newly invented instrumentality. I introduce the concept of invention, as distinguished from discovery and creation, in order to highlight the reciprocal complementary tension and readiness of agent and "material." (The concept of creation would not be inappropriate as long as creation ex nihilo was not implied, but Winnicott's baby is said to be allowed the illusion of having created the maternal breast ex nihilo.)

As commonly used, the word *subjectivity* refers to an individual subject, as agent of spontaneous mental activity that is called into operation by and deals with a world of objects of which it then becomes relatively independent. Most writers on psychoanalysis—beginning with Freud and including such different writers as Melanie Klein, Hartmann, Winnicott, and Kohut, among many others—implicitly or explicitly postulate a separate innate, individual instinctual core or a core self in the infant.[1] Freud's thoughts on the early ego in *Civilization and Its Discontents* (1930), however, deserve close attention:

> The ego detaches itself from the external world. Or, to put it more correctly, originally the ego includes everything, later it separates off an external world from itself. Our present ego-feeling is, therefore, only a shrunken residue of a much more inclusive—indeed an all-embracing—feeling which corresponded to a more intimate bond between the ego and the world about it [the last three words are the translation of the German *Umwelt*]. If we may assume that there are many people in whose mental life this primary ego-feeling has persisted to a greater or less degree, it would exist in them side by side with the narrower and more sharply demarcated ego-feeling of maturity, like a kind of counterpart to it. In that case, the ideational contents appropriate to it would be precisely those of limitlessness and of a bond with the universe—the same ideas with which my friend [Romain Rolland] elucidated the 'oceanic' feeling. (P. 68)

"The ego detaches itself from the external world" or "originally the ego includes everything, later it separates off an external world from itself": Neither way of putting it feels quite right to Freud. I believe

1. I presented parts of my work on sublimation in 1982 to the William Alanson White Psychoanalytic Society of New York. In his discussion of the paper Stephen Mitchell raised searching questions about similarities and differences between Winnicott's and my approach in regard to what has been called the psychological birth of the human infant (Mahler et al. 1975). Although I have been concerned with these and related issues for many years, I am greatly indebted to Stephen Mitchell for having provided new impetus and stimulation to my thoughts on these matters.

this is true because either way implies the differentiation of subject and object. Freud envisions limitlessness and lack of boundaries between ego and world as corresponding to that primary ego-feeling, something all-embracing and—we may add—all-embraced. This "feeling" and "the ideational contents appropriate to it" belong to the stage or level of mentation that is juxtaposed with more "mature" mentation. In Winnicott's transitional phenomena, and a fortiori in the baby's mouth-breast experience, we deal with "these almost intangible quantities" (Freud 1930, p. 72). In Winnicott's "cultural experience" that level of mentation is revived and interdigitates with subsequently developed mental levels. In my view, then, in reference to these early stages we must not think in terms of a subjective instinctual or ego (self) core as opposed to objects.

Several times in this first chapter of *Civilization and Its Discontents*, most vividly at the very end of the chapter, Freud admits that he feels discomfort in dealing with these "obscure modifications of mental life" (p. 73). Discomfort in these realms of mental life is in counterpoise to the discontentment, the *Unbehagen*, in civilization—the avowed topic of the book. It remains for us to try to elucidate further and bring language to these obscure and more or less ineffable regions—a task that Freud started and carried a long way with the invention of his concept of the unconscious. At any rate the twofold discomfort is quite unmistakable and needs to be better understood.[2] In contradistinction to being understood as the inner experience of the

2. I cannot resist the temptation to relate here an anecdote (told to me years ago by Ernst Kris in a personal communication) concerning the title *Das Unbehagen in der Kultur* (translated as *Civilization and Its Discontents*). When the book first appeared in print, some mischievous spirit in Freud's circle turned the title around to read *Das Behagen in der Unkultur*. *Unbehagen* is malaise, discomfort; *Behagen* ease, contentment. *Unkultur* does not only mean absence of culture or civilization but has connotations also of the crude and the vulgar (for example its is a sign of *Unkultur* to swear, and to spit or fart, at least in public); it is uncivilized behavior, something that children and "the lower classes" are prone to indulge in with pleasure. "Civilization and its discontents" became, in the clever title reversal, something like contentment or pleasure in the coarse and unrefined (should one say *unsublimated?*), reflecting, in another way, the discontents of civilization.

individual confronted with the object world, subjectivity may be understood as the creative-destructive spontaneity and power of nature—nature conceived as the *natura naturans* of older philosophers, in contrast to *natura naturata*, which is nature considered as the world of distinct substances or objects. Descartes' *res cogitans* may be taken out of the context of human mentality, where it applies to individual cogitation, and reinterpreted in a wider sense: that of reality, or nature, taken as activity. It would thus contrast with his *res extensa*—nature taken as objective reality, as a (in principle measurable) world of "things" extended in space. In a paradoxical formula: *res cogitans = res extendens versus res extensa = res cogitata*. The present participles in the first equation (*cogitans* and *extendens*) denote activity; the past participles in the second equation (*extensa* and *cogitata*) denote the passive mode of createdness, of "thingness," versus active spontaneity. Individual human mentation, as it develops from the mother-infant matrix, would be but one instance or manifestation of *natura naturans*, of nature's "subjectivity." This subjectivity is vaster, "all-embracing," in comparison to human individual mentation. The dynamic unconscious (Freud's "true psychic reality") is closer to subjectivity understood as nature's activity (Rolland's and Freud's "oceanic feeling") and is the enabling factor, in continuity with nature's subjectivity, for individual mentation and for consciousness. Ultimately it is in individual consciousness that a world of objects and an objective world are presented to a subject; one has no standing without the other. The mechanistic view of nature in scientific materialism carries objectivism to an absurd extreme whereby subjectivity in the just outlined sense is entirely eliminated from the world. Psychoanalytic theory still struggles with this heritage but is in the forefront of efforts to break the hegemony of the modern scientific *natura naturata* interpretation of reality.

It is noteworthy that Freud's last instinct theory—that which describes life (or love) instincts and death (or destructive) instincts—is in keeping with an interpretation of nature as *natura naturans*. He extends the concepts of *Trieb* in such a way that it stands for the spontaneous activity of the universe, of which man's psychosomatic life, and particularly his unconscious, is but one manifestation. He concluded that the two fundamental principles governing "events in the life of the universe and in the life of the mind" as postulated by the pre-Socratic philosopher Empedocles—namely *love* and *strife*— "are, both in name and function, the same as our two primal instincts, Eros and destructiveness."[3]

The "omnipotent creativity" and—as Melanie Klein in particular, has shown us—the destructiveness of the baby do not reside in a primordial individual self or individual instinctual core but in a wider "subjectivity" that includes the creative-destructive powers of the parental couple. Through the activities of parents—each parent a particularized or individuated agent of nature as active power—in the course of time the baby itself becomes such an individuated agent, under favorable circumstances developing a "mind of its own" or self. To my understanding then, the baby's "pure subjectivity" does not mean that the baby is a subject which is allowed the illusion of creating the object *breast*. I suspect that Winnicott would not have disagreed with an interpretation of subjectivity in a wider and different sense, as outlined here, and that he spoke of illusion in this context for want of a less traditional conceptualization.

A last comment on those works of the human imagination—the productions of science, art, philosophy, religious thought and ritual— that are sublimations par excellence, those for which the term, in its nonphysicochemical sense, seems to have been coined. Those we

3. The quotation is from "Analysis Terminable and Interminable" (1937, p. 246; pp. 244 to 247 contain a somewhat detailed discussion of Empedocles and his theory). Other pertinent references may be found in Freud's letter to Einstein entitled "Why War?" (1933, p. 209) and in "An Outline of Psycho-Analysis" (1940, p. 149). In footnote 2 of the latter reference he writes: "This picture of the basic forces or instincts, which still arouses much opposition among analysts, was already familiar to the philosopher Empedocles of Acragas." For further elaboration of the perspectives outlined above, see my paper "Psychoanalysis in Search of Nature," *Annual of Psychoanalysis*, forthcoming.

admire the most hold us spellbound, fill us with awe, partake of magic as they summon and master "secret forces in nature"—our own and those of our surround.[4] Nowadays we seem to acknowledge and yield most readily to the magic of a great work of art. May we assume that this magic is connected with the achievement of a reconciliation—with the return, on a higher level of organization, to the early magic of thought, gesture, word, image, emotion, fantasy, as they become united again with what in ordinary nonmagical experience they only reflect, recollect, represent, or symbolize? Could sublimation be both a mourning of lost original oneness and a celebration of oneness regained?

4. *Webster's New International Dictionary*, 2d ed., s. v. "magic", n.

EPILOGUE

This work is unfinished, a fragment. Here and there passages give the reader to understand that particular aspects and important problems of sublimation need to be taken up at much greater length. The most important problem in this category, to my mind, is the relationship of sublimation to guilt, expiation, and atonement and to celebration and self-liberation, as well as to love and hate—in sum, to the "higher" emotions. They may be called sublimated psychic processes, but, paradoxically, they also may be said to motivate sublimation. Other aspects considered here insufficiently or not at all include the questions of the sublimation of aggressive impulses and of the presumed incompatibility between sublimation and climactic heterosexual fulfillment through intercourse. Not unrelated is the problem of the frequent, hardly coincidental, concomitance of overt homosexuality or bisexuality with creativity. What does sublimation have to do with surplus energy—that is, energy that need no longer be invested in the fight for survival? All these questions and others await further work.

Understanding ourselves, our fellow beings, our world, is sublimation in action. So is the psychoanalytic work that analyst and patient do together. Trying to understand something about sublimation is like trying to pull oneself up by one's own bootstraps. It looks like an imperative urge and an impossible task. As passion wanes, its inner transformation—sublimation—decreases. It is my hope that this book, though a fragment, in some measure conveys a sense of the dialectic of irrationality and rationality, as well as of the dialectic of sham and authenticity, in human life.

REFERENCES

In the list below the dates in parentheses refer to original publication—
either of a work in a foreign language for which the English translation is the
citation of record here or of an essay later collected in the anthology cited. The
Sigmund Freud citations follow a different pattern: The date given is that of
their original publication in German. However, volume citations are to the
Hogarth Press *Standard Edition*.

Fenichel, Otto. 1945. *The Psychoanalytic Theory of Neurosis*. New York: W.
 W. Norton.
Ferenczi, Sandor. (1911) 1950. On Obscene Words. In *Sex in Psychoanalysis*. New York: Brunner.
Freud, Anna. (1936) 1946. *The Ego and the Mechanisms of Defense*. New
 York: International Universities Press.
Freud, Sigmund. *The Standard Edition of the Complete Psychological Works
 of Sigmund Freud*. 24 vols. Ed. James Strachey. London: Hogarth Press,
 1953–74. (Hereafter cited as *S.E.*)
———. 1892–99. Extracts from the Fliess Papers. *S.E.*1.
———. 1900. *The Interpretation of Dreams*. *S.E.*5.
———. 1905. Fragment of an Analysis of a Case of Hysteria. *S.E.*7.
———. 1910a. Five Lectures on Psycho-Analysis. *S.E.*11.
———. 1910b. *Leonardo da Vinci and a Memory of his Childhood*. *S.E.*11.
———. 1910c. The Antithetical Meaning of Primal Words. *S.E.*11.
———. 1912a. The Dynamics of Transference. *S.E.*12.
———. 1912b. Recommendations to Physicians Practising Psycho-Analysis.
 *S.E.*12.
———. 1913a. An Evidential Dream. *S.E.*12.
———. 1913b. *Totem and Taboo*. *S.E.*13.
———. 1914. On Narcissism: An Introduction. *S.E.*14.
———. 1915a. Instincts and Their Vicissitudes. *S.E.*14.
———. 1915b. The Unconscious. *S.E.*14.

————. 1917a. A Metapsychological Supplement to the Theory of Dreams. *S.E.*14.

————. 1917b. Mourning and Melancholia. *S.E.*14.

————. 1920. *Beyond the Pleasure Principle. S.E.*14.

————. 1921. *Group Psychology and the Analysis of the Ego. S.E.*18.

————. 1923a. The Libido Theory. *S.E.*18.

————. 1923b. *The Ego and the Id. S.E.*19.

————. 1924a. The Economic Problem of Masochism. *S.E.*19.

————. 1924b. The Dissolution of the Oedipus Complex. *S.E.*19.

————. 1926. *Inhibitions, Symptoms and Anxiety. S.E.*20.

————. 1927. *The Future of an Illusion. S.E.*21.

————. 1930. *Civilization and Its Discontents. S.E.*21.

————. 1933. Why War? S.E. 22.

————. 1937. Analysis Terminable and Interminable. *S.E.*23.

———— . 1940. An Outline of Psycho-Analysis. *S.E.*23.

————. 1940–68. *Gesammelte Werke.* 18 vols. London: Imago.

Greenacre, Phyllis. 1957. The Childhood of the Artist. *The Psychoanalytic Study of the Child* 12:47–72.

Hartmann, Heinz. 1955. Notes on the Theory of Sublimation. *The Psychoanalytic Study of the Child* 10:9–29.

Jones, Ernest. (1916) 1948. The Theory of Symbolism. In *Papers on Psychoanalysis.* 5th ed. Baltimore: Williams and Wilkins.

Jung, C. G. (1961) 1963. *Memories, Dreams, Reflections.* Trans. Richard and Clara Winston. New York: Pantheon Books.

Keller, Helen. 1903. *The Story of my Life.* New York: Doubleday, Page.

Kris, Ernst. 1955. Neutralization and Sublimation: Observations on Young Children. *The Psychoanalytic Study of the Child* 10:30–46.

Laplanche, J., and Pontalis, J. B. (1967) 1973. *The Language of Psycho-Analysis.* Trans. Donald Nicholson-Smith. New Yorks: W. W. Norton.

Loewald, Hans W. (1955) 1980. Hypnoid State, Repression, Abreaction, and Recollection. In *Papers on Psychoanalysis.* New Haven and London: Yale University Press.

————. (1962) 1980. Internalization, Separation, Mourning, and the Super-ego. In *Papers on Psychoanalysis.*

————. (1971) 1980. Some Considerations on Repetition and Repetition Compulsion. In *Papers on Psychoanalysis.*

———. (1972) 1980. On Motivation and Instinct Theory. In *Papers on Psychoanalysis.*

———. (1973) 1980. On Internalization. In *Papers on Psychoanalysis.*

———. (1975) 1980. Psychoanalysis as an Art and the Fantasy Character of the Psychoanalytic Situation. In *Papers on Psychoanalysis.*

———. (1976) 1980. Perspectives on Memory. In *Papers on Psychoanalysis.*

———. (1978) 1980. Primary Process, Secondary Process, and Language. In *Papers on Psychoanalysis.*

———. (1979) 1980. The Waning of the Oedipus Complex. In *Papers on Psychoanalysis.*

———. Psychoanalysis in Search of Nature. In *Annual of Psychoanalysis.* Forthcoming.

Mahler, M., Pine, F., and Bergman, A. 1975. *The Psychological Birth of the Human Infant.* New York: Basic Books.

Milner, Marion. 1952. Aspects of Symbolism in Comprehension of the Not-Self. *International Journal of Psychoanalysis* 33:181–95.

Piaget, Jean. 1945. *La Formation du Symbole chez l'Enfant.* Neuchatel and Paris: Delachaux & Niestlé.

Rank, Otto, and Sachs, Hanns. (1913) 1916. *The Significance of Psychoanalysis for the Mental Sciences.* Trans. Charles R. Payne. New York: Nervous and Mental Diseases Publishing Co.

Rapaport, David. 1967. A Theoretical Analysis of the Superego Concept. In *The Collected Papers of David Rapaport.* Ed. Merton Gill. New York and London: Basic Books.

Rodrigué, E. 1956. Notes on Symbolism. *International Journal of Psychoanalysis* 37:147–58.

Séchehaye, Marguerite-A. (1947) 1951a. *Symbolic Realization.* New York: International Universities Press.

———. (1950) 1951b. *Reality Lost and Regained: Autobiography of a Schizophrenic Girl.* New York: Grune and Stratton.

Silberer, Herbert. (1912) 1951. On Symbol Formation. In *Organization and Pathology of Thought: Selected Sources.* Translation and commentary by David Rapaport. New York: Columbia University Press.

Strachey, James. 1934. The Nature of the Therapeutic Action of Psycho-Analysis. *International Journal of Psychoanalysis* 15:127–59.

REFERENCES

Webster's New International Dictionary of the English Language. 2d ed. 1958. Springfield, Mass.: G. and C. Merriam Co.

Werner, Heinz, and Kaplan, Bernard. (1963) 1964. *Symbol Formation.* New York: John Wiley and Sons.

Winnicott, Donald W. 1953. Transitional Objects and Transitional Phenomena. *International Journal of Psychoanalysis* 34:89–97.

———. 1967. The Location of Cultural Experience. *International Journal of Psychoanalysis* 48:368–72.

INDEX

aim inhibition, 25–26
Analysis Terminable and Interminable (Freud), 31n9, 80n3
"Antithetical Meaning of Primal Words, The" (Freud), 58n6

Beyond the Pleasure Principle (Freud), 16, 19n3

civilization, 6–7, 6n3, 78n2; and sublimation, 19; and the ego, 20
Civilization and its Discontents (Freud), 16, 17, 77, 78–79
conversion, defined, 13

da Vinci, Leonardo, 9–10, 21
defense, 3–4, 42n1; defined, 4–5; sublimation as, 35–41
desexualization: sublimation as, 19
"Dynamics of Transference, The" (Freud), 59n7

"Economic Problem of Masochism, The" (Freud), 27–28
ego: depth psychology of, 16; and libido, 17, 19; and psychic energy, 21; and instinct, 27; and sublimation, 41–42; relation to world, 77–78

Ego and the Id, The (Freud), 16, 17, 18
Empedocles, 80, 80n3
eros, 11–12, 16, 30; and narcissistic libido, 19; desexualized, 20
"Evidential Dream, An" (Freud), 62

Fenichel, Otto, 3–4, 6, 42, 55
Fleiss, Wilhelm, 1
Fleiss papers, 1
Freud, Anna, 40
Freud, Sigmund, 2, 8, 9, 11, 21, 46; and sexuality, 11n3, 14, 43; on primary narcissism, 16–17; on ego-ideal formation, 18; on superego formation, 18 on desexualization, 19; on desexualized Eros, 20; instinct theory of, 17–18, 21, 25–30, 31n10, 33–35, 36, 44, 79–80; on symbolism, 45, 54–55, 62; on primary ego-feeling, 77–78
"Future of an Illusion, The" (Freud), 69–70

genitals, 10, 11, 13, 26
Greenacre, Phyllis, 21
Group Psychology and the Analysis of the Ego (Freud), 16, 18, 25

87

reality principle, 28–30
"Representation by Symbols in Dreams" (Freud), 62
repression, 36, 37–38; defined, 41–42; and symbolism, 49, 53–55

Sachs, Hans, and Rank, Otto, 46
Séchehaye, M.-A., 58–59
selfobject, 25
sexuality: and the divine, 11–12
Silberer, Herbert, 46
Stekel (Wilhelm), 46
Story of My Life, The (Keller), 62–63
subjectivity, 79–80
sublimation, 1, 5–6, 7–8, 16, 38–39, 82; and cultural pursuits, 1, 74–75, 75n2, 80–81; defined, 3–4, 12–14; and sexual instinct, 5–6; and civilization, 6–7, 19–20; organic, 7; and passion, 9; and eros, 11–12; and metapsychological theory, 15–25; and narcissism, 16–18; desexualization and, 19; and internalization, 19–20; and polarity, 20–22, 23–24; and neutralization, 20–21, 30; manic element of, 22, 24; and the mother-infant matrix, 22–25, 22n5; and differentiation, 24; and aim inhibition, 25–26, 29; as reconciliatory, 33; as defense, 36–37, 41–42, 50; and repression, compared, 37–38, 41–42; and psychoanalytic treatment, 39;

and reaction-formation, compared, 39–40; and psychoanalysis as science, 42; characteristics of, 43; influence of the ego in, 44; and symbolism, 45–47, 49, 50–51
symbolism, 45–46, 52, 61–62; and psychoanalytic theory, 46–47, 49, 50, 53–57; words and, 47–48, 49–50, 57–58, 60; emotions and, 48–49; and repression, 49, 53–55, 58; and defense, 51; defined, 52–53, 66; and language, 53, 57–58; and protosymbolism, 55–56; and psychotherapy, 56–57, 59–60; and religion, 59n7, 72; and illusion, 66–70, 70–75; and transitional objects, 71–72, 75n2
symbolization. See symbolism

Totem and Taboo (Freud), 16
"Transitional Objects and Transitional Phenomena" (Winnicott), 22–25, 70–75

"Unconscious, The" (Freud), 29, 54–55

Werner, Heinz, and Kaplan, Bernard, 50, 61, 62, 63–64
"Why War?" (Freud), 80
Winnicott, Donald, 22–25, 30–31, 70–75, 77, 80